ONE BIG STORY

DISCOVER GOD'S PURPOSES IN HIS WORD

CONTENTS

INTRODUCTION	VI
FAMILY DEVOTIONS	VIII

OLD TESTAMENT ... 1

1. God's Story Begins: Creation ... 2
2. Man's Fall: Adam and Eve ... 3
3. God's Command Restated: Noah ... 4
4. God's Command Ignored: Tower of Babel ... 5
5. God's Promise Put in Motion: Abraham ... 6
6. God's Promise Passed Down: Isaac ... 7
7. God's Promise Passed Down Again: Jacob ... 8
8. God's People Go to Egypt: Joseph ... 9
9. God's Glory Proclaimed: Moses and Pharaoh ... 10
10. God's Power Demonstrated: Red Sea Crossing ... 11
11. God's Purpose for Israel: Kingdom of Priests ... 12
12. God's Decrees for Israel: Loving the Foreigner ... 13
13. A Gentile Declaration: Rahab ... 14
14. Entering God's Promised Land: Crossing the Jordan ... 15
15. A Kinsman Redeemer: Ruth and Boaz ... 16
16. A Young Boy's Refusal: David and Goliath ... 17
17. House for All Nations: The Temple ... 18
18. The World Comes: Solomon and the Queen of Sheba ... 19
19. A Commander's Heart Changed: Naaman, Elisha, and a Servant Girl ... 20
20. Songs of Purpose: The Psalms ... 21
21. Refusal to Share Overruled: Jonah ... 22
22. God's Larger Purpose: Isaiah ... 23
23. A King's Declaration: Daniel and Darius ... 24
24. Future of Nations Foretold: The Prophets ... 25

NEW TESTAMENT 26

25. The Savior is Born: Jesus 27
26. About His Father's Business: Jesus' Childhood 28
27. A Jewish Rejection: Jesus' Public Reading 29
28. Fishers of Men: Jesus' Disciples 30
29. A Confused Teacher Redirected: Nicodemus 31
30. Encountering the Savior of the World: The Samaritan Woman 32
31. Jesus Heals Gentiles: Centurion's Servant 33
32. Jesus Heals Gentiles: Demon-Possessed Man 34
33. Jesus' Sending Strategy: The Twelve and The Seventy 35
34. Jesus' Double Miracle: Feeding 5,000 and 4,000 36
35. A Shepherd's Flock: Other Sheep 37
36. Promise of the Church: Peter 38
37. God's Temple Misused: Jesus Clears the Courts 39
38. Greeks Seeking a Visit: Jesus Predicts His Death 40
39. A Debt is Paid: Jesus' Death and Resurrection 41
40. The Great Commission: Jesus' Last Words 42
41. Outpouring of God's Spirit: Pentecost 43
42. Purposeful Persecution: Believers Scattered 44
43. Samaritans Receive the Spirit: Philip 45
44. A Light to the Gentiles: Paul 46
45. Gentiles Receive God's Spirit: Cornelius and Peter 47
46. Gentile Realization: Peter and Barnabas 48
47. Gospel Decisions: Jerusalem Council 49
48. The Unknown God: Paul in Athens 50
49. Gospel Multiplies Throughout the Gentile World: Paul and Timothy . 51
50. Believer's Responsibility: Paul's Epistles 52
51. A New Kingdom of Priests: Our Part in God's Story 53
52. The Purchase and the Promise: The End of the Story 54

BIBLE CHARACTER CUTOUTS & MEMORY VERSES 56

GOD'S STORY

- ADAM & EVE
- ABRAHAM
- JOSEPH
- MOSES
- RUTH
- JESUS
- DISCIPLES
- PAUL
- YOU & ME!
- CELEBRATION BEFORE THE THRONE!

INTRODUCTION

The Bible is one story ... God's story. Woven throughout is His overarching plan—to make His name great so that people from every nation, tribe, and tongue might know and worship Him.

God set His plan in motion before the creation of the world and will see it through to completion. The exciting thing is that God's story is still unfolding in our day and God invites our families to be a part of it.

As parents, you have the privilege of communicating God's story to your children. This resource gives you a model for sharing God's Word with your family in an engaging, ongoing way that consistently shapes their view of God—His character, His heart, and His purposes—as well as their view of themselves—their identity, their blessings, and their purpose.

HOW DOES THIS WAY OF TEACHING GOD'S WORD BENEFIT YOUR CHILDREN?

1. Children develop a biblical worldview where God is central. They learn that they exist for God, to bring Him glory, not the other way around. This understanding leads to a strong, secure identity as characters in God's story who are deeply loved and called into the service of the eternal King.

2. Tracing how God was at work throughout Bible times shapes how children view all of history. They learn that world events are not random, but an intentional strategy of God to advance His purposes. This understanding provides children with a new lens for looking both at current events and situations in their own lives.

3. As children discover a biblical pattern of God blessing His people for the greater purpose of blessing the nations, they gain a balanced perspective on why God blesses them. This understanding will influence both their attitudes and choices about how they leverage their time, talent, and resources.

4. As children observe how God used Bible characters in every generation to advance His purposes, they begin to view their individual purpose in light of God's plan. Knowing that God has a valuable role for them gives children confidence and direction. Their desire to be a part of something bigger than themselves is satisfied as they join with God in what reaching the nations looks like for their generation.

RESOURCE OVERVIEW

One Big Story has three components that complement one another.

1. A set of 52 **Family Devotions** to help your family trace God's global heart and purposes throughout Scripture and discover your part in God's story.

2. A downloadable set of Bible **character cutouts** that match the Family Devotions. These serve as a visual reminder of how God invites people to join in His ongoing story. *Download at weavefamily.org/StoryActivities*

3. A downloadable set of 24 **memory verses** focused on God's global purposes to help your children develop a heart for the nations. *Download a set in card format at weavefamily.org/StoryActivities*

FAMILY DEVOTIONS

Each Family Devotion includes background information about the Bible passage, a related family activity, discussion questions, and a prayer prompt.

Ideas for using the Family Devotions

Do one Family Devotion each week to develop a habit of studying God's Word in an ongoing way. There are 52 stories, which means you can read one a week for a year!

Background information—the first paragraph of each page—is for you as parents, but if you have older children, feel free to include some of the information to introduce or teach the devotion.

 **FAMILY ACTIVITY**

Include everyone in the family activity. Learning comes through doing!

 BIBLE PASSAGES

Introduce each Bible passage in a way that reinforces that God is the main character of the Bible. Use words similar to this: "Today, we are going to read another part of God's story. I wonder how God will use a boy named David."

Read the Bible passage to your family aloud. If your children are good readers, divide the passage into smaller sections and take turns.

 DISCUSS

Make sure to discuss both questions. They are designed to draw out God's purpose and help you apply the principles to your own family.

 PRAY

Use the prayer prompt to talk to God as a family. Be sensitive to ways God begins to answer your prayers.

OLD TESTAMENT

1. God's Story Begins
CREATION

God's story begins. Before the creation of the world, He existed. By merely speaking, He created the world we live in … every plant, animal, and star in the sky. Then God created man and woman in His own image. As humans, neither Adam nor Eve looked like God, but they both reflected who God is. Humans were unique because God created them to have a special relationship with Him and to share in His purpose to one day be worshiped by all peoples. As part of this purpose, God gave them the command to "be fruitful and multiply, fill the earth and subdue it" (Genesis 1:28). God's original desire was to see humans who reflected His image filling the world so that His glory would cover the earth.

BEGIN BY READING WITH YOUR FAMILY:

Genesis 1:1-28

FAMILY ACTIVITY

Teaching Time: 8 minutes
Materials: Adam and Eve cutouts (optional), mirror

Have family members take turns looking at their own reflection in a mirror. Then sit in a circle so you can see each other. Discuss similarities and differences in your appearance.

DISCUSS

1. God created people all around the world. How can people who look so different from each other all bear the image of God, reflecting who God is? Read Psalm 34:3. What is our purpose as image bearers of God?

2. Mirrors reflect our physical image, but our words and actions reflect our heart. When people look at our family's life, what do our words and actions reflect about God?

PRAY

When God looks across the world, He sees people of all cultures who bear His image. Pray that God will receive the glory among all nations.

2. Man's Fall
ADAM AND EVE

Adam and Eve chose to disobey God by eating from the fruit of the tree of good and evil. Their willful defiance broke their relationship with Him. As a result of their sin, God pronounced punishment on the serpent and both the man and woman. At the same time, God also provided hope for the human race. While the serpent would bruise the heel of the woman's offspring, this offspring would ultimately crush the head of the serpent (Genesis 3:15). This promise refers to Jesus, the one who would one day come to earth as Savior of the World! The broken relationship between man and God will be fixed by God himself.

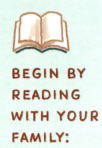

BEGIN BY READING WITH YOUR FAMILY:

Genesis 3

FAMILY ACTIVITY

Teaching Time: 15 minutes
Materials: Adam and Eve cutouts (optional), objects that are broken and tools that can repair them. Use the suggested items or others of your choice: sheet of paper ripped in half/ tape; clothing with a hole or rip/needle and thread; chipped or cracked plate, cup, vase/glue; battery operated toy/batteries.

Spread out the items and tools in separate piles on a table or on the floor. Show how each item has been broken or torn. Let your children match each broken object with the best tool to fix it. Talk about what would happen if you tried to fix the broken glass with the needle and thread or if you tried to repair the hole in the clothes with tape.

DISCUSS

1. Think about the Bible passage we read. What was broken between God and Adam and Eve? God knew the best way to fix the broken relationship. Read Romans 5:10. How did Jesus restore the broken relationship between God and His people?

2. Read 2 Corinthians 5:19-20. How does God want our family to respond to what Jesus has done for us?

PRAY

Many people in our world today do not know about God's promise to Adam and Eve or its fulfillment. Pray that they will hear about Jesus, the only one who can restore their broken relationship with God.

# God's Command Restated
NOAH

Sin grew. During Noah's time, mankind was evil in every way, but God took notice of Noah and counted him righteous. God commanded Noah to build an ark. All of mankind, except Noah and his family, was wiped out in the flood. After the flood, God gave a rainbow as a sign of promise that He would never destroy people in this way again. God gave Noah the same command He had given Adam and Eve… "be fruitful and multiply, fill the earth and subdue it" (Genesis 9:1). God's original plan for the peoples of the earth to reflect their Creator and give Him glory was not derailed by the flood and subsequent destruction of sinful mankind. The promised seed, the Savior, would continue through Noah's son, Shem, and his descendants.

BEGIN BY READING WITH YOUR FAMILY:

Genesis 6:5-9; 7:11-24; 8:1-4, 13-19; 9:1, 12-17

 FAMILY ACTIVITY

Teaching Time: 12 minutes
Materials: Noah cutout (optional), large bowl, lots of dried beans, rice, or unpopped popcorn, colored marker

Before the activity, color one bean, rice grain, or popcorn kernel with a marker and hide it inside a large bowl of many. Have children take turns searching for and finding the one that is different from all the rest. Discuss the state of the world in Noah's time. Explain that although the entire human race was evil, God knew about Noah and did not overlook him or his family.

 DISCUSS

1. Read Genesis 6:8-9. What did God see in Noah that set him apart from all the people on the earth? Was Noah perfect? Read Genesis 1:28 and 9:1. How did God's repeated command link Noah to Adam and Eve? God's promise of a coming Savior continued through Noah's family and his descendants.

2. Read 2 Chronicles 16:9a and 1 Peter 2:9. What kinds of people is God looking for today? If God looks for hearts like Noah's, hearts that are fully committed to Him, what would He see in our family?

 PRAY

Pray that God will cultivate within our family hearts that are fully committed to Him.

 # God's Command Ignored
TOWER OF BABEL

After the flood, the world population increased, but people did not fill the earth as God had commanded. Instead, they decided to live close together and make a name for themselves (Genesis 11:4). They chose their own glory over God's. At that time, all people spoke the same language, making communication easy. Working together, they began constructing a magnificent tower. God came down to earth and confused the language of the people so they could no longer understand one another. The scattering that resulted was in line with God's purpose to have mankind fill the earth so that He might one day receive worship from all peoples. Genesis 10 lists the 70 nations that were created. This was the beginning of nations and people groups as we know them today.

BEGIN BY READING WITH YOUR FAMILY:

Genesis 11:1-8

 ## FAMILY ACTIVITY

Teaching Time: 12 minutes
Materials: None

Stand facing someone in your family. Try these ways of greeting each other.

- Japan – Bow with your hands in front, palms together, like you are praying. Say, "koh-**nee**-chee-wah."
- Bangladesh – Salute with your right hand. Say, "sah-**lahm**."
- Kazakhs (**kah**-zahks) of Central Asia – Put your right hand over your heart and bow slightly. Say, "sah-**lehm**."
- Yao (yahw) of Africa – Clasping the bottom of your right elbow with your left hand, shake hands with your partner. Say, "soo-buh-**yee**-dee."
- Maor (mah-**ohr**) of New Zealand – Press your noses together while closing your eyes. Say, "Kee-**ohr**."
- Northern Mozambique – Clap your hands three times. Say, "sah-**lah**-mah."

 ## DISCUSS

1. Share about a time you heard someone speaking a different language or saw words written in a different language. How did different languages begin?

2. Read Malachi 1:11. Why did God want people to spread out around the world? Even though the people at Babel refused to scatter willingly, how did God make sure that His plan was accomplished? How can our family spread God's name and make Him famous?

 ## PRAY

Pray that people from every language group will have the opportunity to hear about Jesus.

5 God's Promise Put in Motion
ABRAHAM

Many years after Babel, God chose to speak to Abram (later called Abraham), a man who lived in Haran. God called him to leave his home and go to a land that God would show him. God made an everlasting covenant with Abraham, an unbreakable promise, that would be pivotal throughout human history. God would bless Abraham so that he would be a blessing, the same purpose God has in blessing His people today. God would also form the nation of Israel from Abraham's family. Most importantly, God declared to Abraham, "in you all the families of the earth will be blessed" (Genesis 12:3). Jesus, the Savior of the world and ultimate fulfillment of the promise to bless all the families of the earth, would come through Abraham's line.

BEGIN BY READING WITH YOUR FAMILY:

Genesis 12:1-3; 17:5-8, 19; 22:17-18

FAMILY ACTIVITY

Teaching Time: 12 minutes
Materials: Abraham cutout (optional), small bags of treats for one third of the people in your family. Put enough treats inside for everyone to get a treat if those receiving treat bags share. For example, if you have 6 people in your family, fix two bags with enough treats for six people.

After dinner, tell your family that you have prepared treats for them. Begin passing out the treat bags and apologize for running out of bags. Discuss ways to make sure that everyone receives a treat. Have those who received bags share treats with those who did not. Explain that God blessed Abraham and his family was so that he would bless others around him.

Option: For small families, use stuffed animals or dolls in this demonstration, invite friends to join you, or do this activity with a group from church.

DISCUSS

1. If you did not receive a treat bag, how did that feel? If you did receive a treat bag, was it because you did something to deserve it? Did God bless Abraham because God loved him more than the other people living around him? Did Abraham do something special to receive God's favor? What did God expect Abraham to do with his blessings?

2. In our world today, one third of people have never had the opportunity to learn about God's gift of salvation through Jesus. Our family knows and loves Jesus. Why did God bless our family in this way? What blessings (material things, talents, knowledge, experiences, spiritual life) do our family have that we could pass on to other people?

PRAY

Pray that believers worldwide would actively seek to participate in God's purposes to bless all the families of the earth.

6 God's Promise Passed Down
ISAAC

God's covenant promise was for Abraham and his offspring (Genesis 22:18). God's blessing was passed down to Abraham's son, Isaac. God commanded Isaac to stay in the land promised to him, even during a great famine. Despite Isaac's fear and opposition from neighboring herdsmen, he obeyed in faith. God repeated His promise afresh to Isaac, assuring him of His presence, blessing, and purpose... "through your offspring, all nations on earth will be blessed" (Genesis 26:4).

BEGIN BY READING WITH YOUR FAMILY:

Genesis 25:11; 26:1-6, 12-25

FAMILY ACTIVITY

Teaching Time: 12 minutes
Materials: Isaac cutout (optional), squares of paper, scissors

Make your own paper snowflakes or follow these directions:

1. Fold the paper square in half to form a rectangle.
2. Fold in half again to form a square.
3. Rotate the square to make a diamond shape. The tip corresponding to the paper's center (when unfolded) should be pointing downwards.
4. Fold the paper in half vertically to form a triangle.
5. Keeping the paper folded, cut away shapes along the edges.
6. Unfold the paper. Look at your creation.

DISCUSS

1. When did you see your snowflake's full design—before or after you unfolded the paper? What happened to the small number of cuts you made around the outside of the paper? God did not show Abraham or Isaac the full picture of how He would bless all the families of the earth through them. What are some ways that Abraham and Isaac were obedient to the small part that God did show them? Their faithful actions had an impact on many, many future generations, including ours.

2. Look at your snowflake creations and discuss how they are different. In nature, every snowflake is unique. In the same way, God has a unique role for each of us and for our family. Are we willing to live it out?

PRAY

Ask God to reveal your family's unique role in His purposes and give you willing hearts to respond.

 # God's Promise Passed Down Again
JACOB

Isaac had twin sons, Jacob and Esau. God chose to continue His covenant through Jacob, the younger son. Instead of trusting in God's ways and timing, Jacob tried to gain the promised blessing through deception. After Isaac blessed Jacob, Esau threatened to kill him. Jacob ran for his life. Frightened, alone, and desperate, Jacob had come to the end of himself. At this point, God renewed the blessing. God repeated to Jacob the promises He had made to both Abraham and Isaac: "All peoples on earth will be blessed through you and your offspring" (Genesis 28:14).

BEGIN BY READING WITH YOUR FAMILY:

Genesis 27:6-37, 41-45; 28:10-15

 ## FAMILY ACTIVITY

Teaching Time: 12 minutes
Materials: Jacob cutout (optional), eight strips of paper to form links of a chain, pencil or marker, tape or stapler

Work together to make a paper chain. Take three strips of paper and write one of the following names on each strip: Abraham, Isaac, and Jacob. Use tape or staples to create three links and attach them in order. Explain how God passed His promised blessing down through families and that His promise was not only for Abraham, but also for his children, grandchildren, and all the children who would be born after him. Work together to construct another chain that reflects your family. On the first strip write the names of your children's grandparents. On the second strip write your own (parents) names. On the third strip, write, or let your children write, their names. On the last strip, write "next generation." Create four links and attach them in order to form a second chain. As you do this, share how God still passes His blessing down through families who love and obey Him in our day. On the remaining strip of paper, write "Jesus." As you attach the "Jesus" link after the "Jacob" link, explain that Jesus was born into the family of Abraham. Read Galatians 3:7 and 3:29 and use these verses to explain how our faith in Jesus connects us to Abraham's family. Demonstrate this by connecting the two chains with the "Jesus" link in the middle.

 ## DISCUSS

1. What did Abraham pass on to his son, Isaac? When Isaac was a father, what did he pass on to his son, Jacob? Share with you children, some of the most important things your parents (their grandparents) taught you? Let your children share some important things you have taught them about God.

2. Read Genesis 28:14b. Put your family's name in the verse. How is your family blessed by the fulfillment of God's promise to Abraham? How can your family be a part of God's promise to bless all the nations?

 ## PRAY

Ask God to show your family practical ways to join with Him in blessing the nations.

God's People Go to Egypt
JOSEPH

Jacob's family grew. His sons would one day form the 12 tribes of Israel, the nation through whom the promised Savior would come. During a time of great famine, God used Jacob's son, Joseph, to move their entire family to Egypt and save them from starvation. When Joseph grew old, he said to his brothers, "I am about to die. But God will surely come to your aid and take you up out of this land, to the land he promised on oath to Abraham, Isaac and Jacob, and then you must carry my bones up from this place" (Genesis 50:24-26). Joseph understood that God's promised blessing would continue through Abraham's family line. God's plan was not hindered by present circumstances or location.

BEGIN BY READING WITH YOUR FAMILY:

Genesis 45:1-11; 46:2-7; 50:20-25

FAMILY ACTIVITY

Teaching Time: 12 minutes
Materials: Joseph cutout (optional), shallow basin of water, newspaper or paper towels

Spread newspaper on the floor next to the basin of water. Have one child leave the room. Take turns stepping into the water with bare feet and making footprints on the paper. Have the child return and invite him to identify each set of footprints. Choose a different child to leave the room. As you make footprints this time, pick up one of your children and make footprints while carrying him. Invite the child who left the room to guess who was standing on the paper. Discuss the trick and connect it to the story of Joseph. Explain that just like in the activity, God carried Joseph through the hard times. Discuss what some of these hard times were. Explain that even though Joseph endured many difficulties in his life, he was never alone.

Option: For small families, invite friends to join you, or do this activity with a group from church.

DISCUSS

1. Which part of the activity was like God's carrying Joseph? What was God's greater purpose in bringing Joseph to live in Egypt? (Genesis 50:19-21)

2. Describe a difficult time in your life when you realized God was carrying you. How might God want to use our difficult circumstances in the lives of unbelievers?

PRAY

Ask God to give your family the faith to trust that God is working out His plans even through difficult circumstances.

God's Glory Proclaimed
MOSES AND PHARAOH

In Egypt, Jacob's descendants grew to a nation of 2-3 million people. To gain control over the Israelites (or Hebrews), Egypt's leader enslaved them and treated them harshly. Through Moses, God set about freeing His people. When Pharaoh refused to let them go, God sent ten plagues to strike the Egyptians' water supply, crops, animals, and families. God declared that through the plagues, the whole world would know the mighty hand of the Lord. After the final plague of the firstborn, Pharaoh let the Israelites go. As they fled Egypt, many others went with them, wanting to be a part of God's people (Exodus 12:38). These were probably Egyptians who had seen the wonders of Israel's God and believed.

BEGIN BY READING WITH YOUR FAMILY:

Exodus 6:6-8; 9:16; 12:38

FAMILY ACTIVITY

Teaching Time: 10 minutes
Materials: Moses cutout (optional)

Invite family members to demonstrate one way they are physically strong (running, jumping, arm wrestling, lifting something heavy). Talk about Olympic events in which athletes demonstrate physical strength. Discuss the difference in scope between being a winner in your family and taking first prize in the Olympics. Share that one of God's purposes in sending the plagues on the Egyptians was to show the whole world that He is God Almighty (Exodus 9:16). Each plague was like an Olympic event in which God proved Himself more powerful than Pharaoh and all the Egyptian gods and goddesses. Read Exodus 12:38 and share that as a result of God's demonstration of power, other people living in Egypt were attracted to the true God and chose to join the Israelites when they left Egypt.

DISCUSS

1. How did God demonstrate His power in Egypt? What was one result of God's demonstration of power? (see Exodus 12:38)

2. In what ways does God demonstrate His power in our lives today? How can our family share God's power to save with people who do not know Jesus?

PRAY

Ask God to use your family to attract unbelievers to Himself.

# 10 God's Power Demonstrated
RED SEA CROSSING

As the Israelites traveled towards the Red Sea, Pharaoh pursued them. Finding themselves trapped between Pharaoh's army and a huge body of water, God's people cried out to Him in terror. God told Moses that He would demonstrate His power so that "the Egyptians will know that I am the Lord when I gain glory through Pharaoh, his chariots and his horsemen" (Exodus 14:18). God miraculously parted the waters, allowing the Israelites to cross over on dry land. But Pharaoh's army drowned as the waters flowed back. News of Israel's powerful God spread to Gentile people in Canaan who said "we have heard how the Lord dried up the water of the Red Sea for you when you came out of Egypt" (Joshua 2:10).

BEGIN BY READING WITH YOUR FAMILY:

Exodus 14:10-18, 21-31; Joshua 2:8-11

 ## FAMILY ACTIVITY

Teaching Time: 10 minutes
Materials: Moses cutout (optional); bucket, tub, sink, or pool; water

Fill a large bucket, bathtub, sink, or small pool with water. Challenge your children to part the water. Be creative—use your hands, tools, containers, toys, etc.

 ## DISCUSS

1. Were you able to part the waters? Is it possible for human hands? What kind of power would it take to do it?

2. Read Exodus 14:13-18 and Joshua 2:11. What was God's greater purpose for parting the Red Sea?

 ## PRAY

Ask God to demonstrate His power in your family in a way that draws unbelievers to Him.

God's Purpose for Israel
KINGDOM OF PRIESTS

The Israelites camped near Mount Sinai. On the mountain, God gave their leader, Moses, a promise to pass on to the people. Out of all nations, they would be God's treasured possession. God also gave them a purpose: to be a kingdom of priests and a holy nation. Through the Israelites, God would continue to fulfill His covenant promise to Abraham to bless all the nations of the earth. God's laws, including the Ten Commandments, would prepare Israel for life in the land they were entering. By observing these laws, Israel would show their wisdom and understanding to the surrounding nations. As these nations observed the close relationship between God and His people, they would be drawn to Him.

BEGIN BY READING WITH YOUR FAMILY:

Exodus 19:1-8; Deuteronomy 4:5-8

FAMILY ACTIVITY

Teaching Time: 15 minutes
Materials: Nation of Israel cutout (optional), treat that will fit in your pocket (candy, gum, etc.), five pieces of paper with arrows drawn on them

Beforehand, hide the treat in your pocket. Inform your children that a small treasure is hidden in the room and give them two minutes to hunt for it. When they cannot find it, offer to make the hunt easier. Ask them to leave the room until you call them. Use four arrow signs to make a path across the floor leading toward the parent with the treat. Hold up the remaining sign so that the arrow points directly at the pocket holding the treat. Invite the children to return and look for the treasure again. When they find it, enjoy eating the treat. Discuss why it was easier to find the treasure the second time. Talk about the treasure that the people of Israel brought with them as they entered Canaan—the knowledge of the one true God. When God called the people of Israel a kingdom of priests, He was identifying their purpose. They were not to hide their treasure from the people in the land, but to act as arrows, pointing them to the true God.

DISCUSS

1. Read 1 Peter 2:9. Peter wrote this passage to believers. As believers, how is our purpose similar to the purpose God gave the people of Israel? According to this verse, what should be our motivation for sharing Jesus with others?

2. In what ways can our family point other people to God?

PRAY

Ask God to make your family like arrows that point others to God Almighty.

 # God's Decrees for Israel
LOVING THE FOREIGNER

Woven throughout God's decrees for Israel were reminders of His love for the foreigners residing among His people. God made it clear the He showed no partiality. Foreigners were to be included in the joyous celebration of the Jewish festivals. God also made sure foreigners were provided for. Every three years, God's people gave a tithe to provide food not only for for the Levite priests, but also for the foreigners. At harvest time, the people were commanded to leave what remained in their fields for the foreigner to glean. God desired that His people love, provide for, and reach out to those around them who did not know Him.

BEGIN BY READING WITH YOUR FAMILY:

Deuteronomy 10:17-19; 14:28-29; 16:14; 24:17-22

 ### FAMILY ACTIVITY

Teaching Time: 1 hour, ongoing
Materials: Nation of Israel cutout (optional)

Connect the foreigners in these Bible passages to modern-day immigrants and refugees in your community. Explain that when immigrant and refugee families arrive in a new region, they lack many things needed to begin their new life. Imagine moving to another country or area with nothing but the clothes you are wearing and what you can carry. What might you need to set up a new home, feed and clothe your family, and go to a new school? Investigate ways your family can help immigrants or refugees living in your area. Ask a leader at your local church for ideas. Visit a Christian ministry in your area that is serving refugee and immigrant populations and see how you may be able to partner with them. Plan a family activity to help refugees or immigrants. Think about how you might continue to serve them on an ongoing basis.

 ### DISCUSS

1. In Old Testament times, what were two ways God used His people to care for the needy foreigners living among them? (see Deuteronomy 14:28-29 and 24:19-22)

2. Why do you think God wants us to bless immigrant and refugee families in our community?

 ### PRAY

Ask God to give your family His compassionate heart for immigrants and refugees in your area.

13 A Gentile Declaration
RAHAB

Stories of what Israel's powerful God did to the Egyptians and Amorite kings struck fear in the hearts of surrounding nations. When Israel's leader, Joshua, sent spies into Jericho, they met Rahab, a woman whose response to these same stories was one of faith. She shared what she had heard about Israel's God and acknowledged, "The Lord your God is God in heaven above and on earth below" (Joshua 2:11). Rahab risked her life to protect the spies in return for the chance to be saved from Jericho's destruction and joined with God's people. She was an unlikely candidate—a woman, a prostitute, a non-Jewish foreigner—but the promise to Abraham was passed on through Rahab. This made her the first Gentile in the genealogy of Jesus. God was already blessing the nations!

BEGIN BY READING WITH YOUR FAMILY:

Deuteronomy 20:16-18; Joshua 2

 FAMILY ACTIVITY

Teaching Time: 12 minutes
Materials: Rahab cutout (optional), two of the same kind of fruit or flower that grows on a tree, one different kind of fruit or flower

Set out the three objects and have the children point out the one that is different. Talk about the differences (color, size, shape, texture, taste). Would both kinds of fruit grow on the same plant or come from different plant families? Share that God's promises were passed down through generations of Israelite families. Using the two similar fruits, talk about how these relatives shared the same history, had similar customs, and worshipped the same God. Now hold up the different fruit as you emphasize that Rahab was not part of Israel. She was born into a Canaanite family that worshipped idols, and she grew up in Jericho, a city that God judged for its wickedness. When Rahab responded in faith to what she knew about God, God rescued her and made her a part of His family. Share the joyful news that God accepts each of us in the same way—not because of who we are, but because of our response to who God is.

 DISCUSS

1. Think of ways that Rahab was probably different from the people of Israel. In what important way was she the same? (see Joshua 2:11)

2. Matthew recorded the family line of Jesus, beginning with Abraham. Read Matthew 1:5. Who became one of Jesus' relatives? What can this teach us about God's heart and plan for all peoples?

 PRAY

Thank God for His mercy and grace towards all who put their faith in Jesus.

# Entering God's Promised Land
CROSSING THE JORDAN

As Israel entered the Promised Land, an obstacle stood in their way—the Jordan River. Just as God did at the Red Sea, He parted the waters and provided a way forward. Joshua reminded the people that God's purpose in both miracles was the same—"so that all the peoples of the earth might know that the hand of the Lord is powerful and so that you might always fear the Lord your God" (Joshua 4:24). The people crossed over on dry land and set up rocks taken from the riverbed as a memorial of God's mighty acts on their behalf. After Israel marched around Jericho for seven days, God caused the fortified city to fall. And so, God began to fulfill a second promise to Abraham, to give his descendants a great land.

BEGIN BY READING WITH YOUR FAMILY:

Joshua 3:14-17; Joshua 4

Teaching Time: 15 minutes
Materials: Joshua cutout (optional), 3-4 items that serve as reminders (vacation photo or souvenir, calendar, sticky note, invitation to an event, kitchen timer, clock or phone alarm), rock for each family member, permanent markers.

Show each object (not the rocks) and discuss how it helps us remember important events or things we should do. God wanted the people of Israel to remember that He always keeps His promises. Use one rock to explain that God's special reminders were twelve rocks taken from the Jordan River. These rocks would remind God's people of His powerful ability to care for them. This would be important to remember as Israel entered a new land filled with people and situations they had never encountered. Hand each family member a rock and markers. On each rock, record a way that God has provided for and cared for your family. Pile the rocks in a place where you can easily see them and be reminded of God's greatness and care.

 DISCUSS

1. Read Joshua 4:20-23. Besides being a reminder to the people who witnessed this miracle, how would the pile of rocks be used in the future?

2. What is our family learning about God that we could to pass on to future generations?

 PRAY

Ask God to give your family daily reminders of who He is, especially when He leads you into unknown territory.

 A Kinsman Redeemer
RUTH AND BOAZ

After Joshua's generation, the nation of Israel turned away from God. "In those days there was no king in Israel. Everyone did what was right in his own eyes" (Judges 21:25). A 300-year cycle began in which God brought judgment, Israel repented, and God sent them a deliverer. After enjoying peace, Israel would once again turn away from God. In this dark period, Scripture records the encouraging story of Ruth, a Moabite woman who was attracted to the God of Israel. Ruth gave up her own country and gods to follow her mother-in-law, Naomi, back to the land of Israel. God displayed His faithfulness to this Gentile (non-Jewish) woman through Boaz, an Israelite man who continued to serve God even when others turned away. God's promise to Abraham, to be a blessing for all peoples, was passed to Ruth. She would be the great, great grandmother of King David and an ancestor of Jesus.

BEGIN BY READING WITH YOUR FAMILY:

Ruth 1:6-9, 22; 2:2-12; 3:7-13; 4:9-10, 13-17

 FAMILY ACTIVITY

Teaching Time: 15 minutes
Materials: Ruth and Boaz cutout (optional); 2 identical candles; 1 candle of a different color, size, or shape; matches or lighter
Setting Up: Before you begin, place one of the identical candles (unlit) on the ground in a safe place.

After dark, gather your family for a game of Follow the Leader. Hold the two remaining candles and matches. Light the candle that looks identical to the one you placed on the ground outside. Discuss how Ruth was faced with a choice: going back to her relatives and old way of life or following Naomi into the dark unknown. Even though Ruth did not know the way forward, she trusted Naomi and Naomi's God. Hold up the lit candle representing Naomi, go outside, and lead the way into the darkness. Invite you children to follow you like Ruth did. Make your way towards the candle on the ground. Stop and invite a child to pick it up. Explain that when Naomi and Ruth arrived in Israel, they met Boaz. Most Israelites had turned away from God, but not Boaz. He trusted and followed God. As you light the identical candle representing Boaz, explain that his obedient life was like a light in a dark time of evil. Now hand the different-looking candle to a child. Discuss ways that Ruth was different from Naomi and Boaz. As a Gentile, Ruth had grown up with different customs, including worshipping idols. She left her old life behind and chose to worship the true God. As you light the different-looking candle representing Ruth, talk about how Ruth was a light, too, and how she became part of God's family, even though she was from another people.

 DISCUSS

1. Ruth abandoned her former way of life. What kinds of things might Ruth have seen in the lives of Naomi and Boaz that attracted her so strongly to their God?

2. Read Matthew 5:14-16. How does Jesus describe believers? Why are we to shine? Is there anything about the light of God in our family that would attract other people to follow Jesus?

 PRAY

Ask God to show your family how to shine forth the light of God to people you encounter in your daily lives.

A Young Boy's Refusal
DAVID AND GOLIATH

Before David became a king, he was just a shepherd boy, but God saw in David what He did not see in any of David's older, bigger brothers. David loved the Lord and understood God's heart for all nations to worship Him. Upon arriving at the Israelites' camp, David encountered the sneering Goliath. David would not stand for God's name being profaned among the Gentile (non-Jewish) nations. Too small to even wear the king's battle armor, David took on Goliath with just a few stones. David declared not only that the battle was the Lord's, but that through it, the whole world would know there was a God in Israel (1 Samuel 17:46).

BEGIN BY READING WITH YOUR FAMILY:

1 Samuel 17:4-24, 26, 32-33, 37-51

FAMILY ACTIVITY

Teaching Time: 20 minutes
Materials: David child-sized cutout (optional), measuring tape or ruler, small soft object

Read 1 Samuel 17:4 and explain that David was an average-sized boy and Goliath was a giant man who stood 3 m (9 ft 9 in) tall. Measure or estimate this height. Let each person compare his own height to Goliath's. Share that David was not trained in battle. Goliath had weapons, but David only had stones and a sling. He was not strong enough to wear armor to protect himself. Act out what it might look like to wear or carry something that is too heavy. Explain how it seemed impossible for David to defeat a giant, but God looked past the obvious and saw something in David that He could use for His purpose. David knew of God's sovereignty and power. David was fighting for God's honor and he saw the outcome of the battle as the Lord's. Choose one person to be Goliath and stand 2.5 m (8 ft) away. Have the others be David. Take turns tossing a soft object at Goliath. When Goliath is hit, he must fall down. Switch roles if your have time. Finish the drama with this question and answer:

Parent: Why did David want to fight Goliath?

Children (shout): So the whole world will know there is a God in Israel.

DISCUSS

1. Read 1 Samuel 16:7. How does God view us? How does this change our attitude when God calls us to do something?

2. David could not stand for God's name to be defamed among the nations. His view of God led him to make decisions of courage. How do you feel when you hear others dishonoring God's name in the world? What is your response when you hear these things?

PRAY

Ask God to reveal how your family can be used to proclaim God's name.

 # House for All Nations
THE TEMPLE

David had many children, including Solomon. God chose to pass on His promise to Abraham through him. Solomon had the privilege of building God's temple, a central place of worship for Israel. Inside the temple, an area was designated as the court of the Gentiles. At the dedication of the temple, King Solomon prayed before an assembly of the people. He asked God to hear the prayers not only of Israel, but also of every foreigner who came to pray, so that all the people of the earth would know God. Later, the temple would be called "a house of prayer for all nations" (Isaiah 56:7).

BEGIN BY READING WITH YOUR FAMILY:

1 Kings 8:22-30, 38-43

 ### FAMILY ACTIVITY

Teaching Time: 20 minutes, ongoing
Materials: Solomon cutout (optional), blankets or cardboard boxes, pictures of people from around the world, paper, markers, tape

Use blankets or cardboard boxes to create a temple. Talk about why the Jewish temple had an area set aside for Gentiles. Decorate the inside of your house of prayer with pictures or drawings of people from all around the world. During the week, use this as a place where your family can gather and pray for the nations.

 ### DISCUSS

1. Think about Solomon's prayer. What did Solomon believe about the reach of the Lord's fame and His desire for foreigners?
2. Read Revelation 7:9. How is the temple foreshadowing what is to come?

 ### PRAY

Pray, like Solomon, that all the people of the earth would know God.

18 The World Comes
SOLOMON AND THE QUEEN OF SHEBA

After Solomon became king, the Lord appeared to him in a dream, saying, "Ask for whatever you want me to give you." Solomon's request for wisdom pleased God. God not only gave Solomon a wise and discerning heart, but riches and honor as well (1 Kings 3:12-13). As Solomon became great, leaders from all nations came to listen to his wisdom. The Queen of Sheba heard about Solomon's fame and his relationship to the Lord. She journeyed far to test Solomon with difficult questions. After meeting Solomon and seeing his kingdom, the queen praised God for what He had given Solomon and for His eternal love for Israel.

BEGIN BY READING WITH YOUR FAMILY:

1 Kings 10:1-13, 23-24

 FAMILY ACTIVITY

Teaching Time: over several days
Materials: Solomon cutout (optional), small pieces of paper or index cards, paper punch or scissors, binder ring or string

A few days prior to this activity, seek out 2-4 people of influence in your children's lives that they see on a regular basis (grandparent, teacher, pastor, neighbor) Invite each person to write down a piece of godly wisdom on the sheet of paper or index card that you provide.

As a family, talk about the Queen of Sheba's search for wisdom. Explain that when she heard about Solomon's wisdom, fame, and riches, she traveled great distances to meet him and ask him difficult questions. She discovered that Solomon's wisdom did not come from himself, but from God!

Explain that we can seek godly wisdom, too. Tell your children about the people who have prepared a piece of wisdom to give them. Throughout the week as they see these people, have your children ask them for godly wisdom. Each person should share their piece of godly wisdom and give your child the paper to keep. At the end of the week, gather all of the sheets of paper. Punch a hole in each sheet and put them on a binder ring or tie them together with a string so you can save them.

Option: For younger children, write your own words of wisdom on 2-4 cards and hide them throughout the house. Send your children on a hunt to seek wisdom.

 DISCUSS

1. Read James 1:5. Where do we get wisdom? What type of people should we seek for wisdom?

2. What things happen in the world that cause people to seek godly wisdom? Read 1 Kings 10:9. What might happen if we share godly wisdom with others?

 PRAY

Pray that people around the world seeking answers would turn to godly people for wisdom.

A Commander's Heart Changed
NAAMAN, ELISHA, AND A SERVANT GIRL

Naaman was a man of prestige and a brave soldier, but he was defenseless against the deadly leprosy that wracked his body. God not only chose to heal this Gentile (not Jewish) army commander, but also chose to use a child to point him toward God! Naaman's young servant girl risked her life to proclaim that Elisha, a prophet of God's people, could heal Naaman. Naaman listened as she spoke up in confidence and faith. After traveling to meet Elisha and following his instructions (though reluctantly at first), Naaman was healed! Naaman proclaimed that there was no God in all the world except in Israel (2 Kings 5:15). Not only did Naaman exalt God, but he made a choice to worship Him only.

BEGIN BY READING WITH YOUR FAMILY:

2 Kings 5:1-15

 FAMILY ACTIVITY

Teaching Time: 15 minutes
Materials: Naaman's Servant Girl cutout (optional); cross or Bible; blocks, toy cars, balls, or ramps

Work together to set up the objects close enough to cause a chain reaction (when you move the first object forward, it will bump into the next object and cause it and the remaining objects to move as well). After the last object, place a cross or a Bible to represent Naaman coming to the Lord. Talk about how Naaman was an important soldier who had leprosy, an incurable disease. Who could help heal him? Share how Naaman's servant girl set things in motion when she spoke up in confidence. Invite one of your children to start the chain reaction. As the reaction sets off, explain that because of her faith, Naaman went to the king of Aram who sent him to see Elisha. Next Elisha sent Naaman to the Jordan River where Naaman was healed. This resulted in Naaman making the choice to worship God only. Rejoice that the servant girl's faith caused a chain reaction that pointed Naaman, a Gentile, toward the true God!

 DISCUSS

1. Naaman's servant was a young girl, but God has no age limit for people He chooses to use in His global purposes. Who are some other children God used?

2. Has there been a time when you have seen God set things in motion because of your family's faith?

 PRAY

Pray that God would give your family confidence and faith to point others to Him.

20 Songs of Purpose
THE PSALMS

The Psalms are a collection of songs, prayers, and poems that reflect God's purposes. Written by several authors, primarily King David, the Psalms remind us of God's desire to be worshipped by all nations. Psalm 67 reminds Israel that God did not call them as His own for their own personal benefit and blessing. Instead, the psalmist reminds the people that God's graciousness and blessings come to them so that God's salvation will be known among all nations, so that all the ends of the earth will fear God.

BEGIN BY READING WITH YOUR FAMILY:

Psalm 67; 22:27-28; 46:10; 86:9; 96:1-10

FAMILY ACTIVITY

Teaching Time: 15 minutes
Materials: The Psalmists cutout (optional)

Working together, name ways that members of your family differ from each other (clothing, size, body features). Just like I look different than you, the blessings God gives to me can look different from your blessings. Now think about what is the same about the inside of each family member's body (bones, organs, blood, muscles). Just as we are the same on the inside, God's purpose for blessing each of us is the same. Read Psalm 67:2-5 and discuss God's plan for the peoples of the world. God blesses us so that we can share the good news of Jesus with other people who have not heard yet. Take turns sharing different ways God has blessed each of you. Emphasize that although God's ways of blessing people may be different, God's purpose for blessing stays the same.

DISCUSS

1. Are there places in the world that you know of where people do not fear God? What does it mean to fear God?

2. Read Psalm 67:7 together, but instead of using "us," insert your family's last name. How can we use our blessings to help these people come to know God?

PRAY

Pray Psalm 67:1 as a family.

21 Refusal to Share Overruled
JONAH

God told Jonah to take the gospel to the Assyrians—an extremely wicked people and an enemy of the Jews. At first, Jonah was unwilling to go to Nineveh. He did not want to give an evil Gentile city the opportunity to know and worship God. He knew God was gracious and compassionate, slow to anger, and abounding in love (Jonah 4:2). After his encounter with a "big fish," Jonah finally went to Nineveh and shared about the true God. The Assyrian people heard the message of the Lord, repented, and were shown mercy by God! Jonah's story shows how God continues to demonstrate to His people the greatness of His love and concern for the unreached peoples of the world.

BEGIN BY READING WITH YOUR FAMILY:

Jonah 1:1-17; 2:1,10; 3:3-10; 4:1-4,11

FAMILY ACTIVITY

Teaching Time: 15 minutes
Materials: Jonah cutout (optional); bowl or vase; strainer, colander, or sieve; water

Allow one child to pour water into the bowl. What happened to the water once you poured it? Connect the idea of the bowl's keeping the water in with Jonah's desire to keep God all to himself. Jonah did not want the Assyrians to come to know and worship God.

Emphasize that God had a different plan in mind. Allow another child to pour water into the strainer over the sink. Observe how the water flows through the strainer. Explain that instead of keeping the truth of God to himself, God wanted Jonah to share it with the Assyrian people. Talk about how it is the same for us as believers and how God want us to share Him with others so they can know and worship Him, too!

DISCUSS

1. Have you had a time when you wanted to keep God to yourself? Read 1 Chronicles 16:24. How does keeping God to ourselves go against God's plans for us?

2. Who are some people in your family's life that God may want you to share Him with? What are some ways you can share God with these people?

PRAY

Pray that God would show you new ways to share God with others.

God's Larger Purpose
ISAIAH

With a divided kingdom and a broken people, God sent prophets to His people. Many prophets focused on the coming Messiah, calling Israel to repentance and bringing a message of hope. Isaiah foretold God's global plan long before Christ came. It would be too small a thing for Christ to come only for the lost sheep of Israel. He would also be a light to the Gentiles (non-Jewish peoples). After Jesus' birth, Simeon referenced Isaiah's words when he declared that Jesus was a "light to the Gentiles" (Luke 2:32). Paul also used Isaiah's words to justify his work among the Gentiles: "Therefore we turn to the Gentiles, to preach the gospel to them, because so has the Lord commanded us, saying, 'I have sent you to be a light to the Gentiles'" (Acts 13:47). As God sent Jesus into the world to be a light to all people, so is He sending us (John 20:21)!

BEGIN BY READING WITH YOUR FAMILY:

Isaiah 49:6

FAMILY ACTIVITY

Teaching Time: 15 minutes
Materials: Isaiah cutout (optional), flashlight or candles and matches, world map

Go outside with your family at night, taking a flashlight (or several candles) and a world map. Locate Israel on the map (to the east of Egypt). Hold the flashlight (or one candle) close to the map so that the light focuses on the country of Israel. Read Isaiah 49:6 and move the flashlight further away from the map (or light more candles) so that light shines on the whole world. Explain that in this verse, God shares His big plan for Jesus. Jesus would not be a Savior for Israel only, but for the whole world. Let each child have a turn shining the light on Israel and then on the whole world as your family says this verse together.

DISCUSS

1. What are some characteristics of light? Compare the light to the darkness. How is Jesus like the light? How are we like the light?

2. Read Matthew 5:14-16. Why does God want us to be a light to others?

PRAY

Pray that those who are in darkness would see the light of life in Jesus.

23 A King's Declaration
DANIEL AND DARIUS

When God's people lived as exiles in Babylon, God continued to proclaim His name in this foreign land. Daniel was a believer in the true God. Highly respected in the eyes of King Darius, Daniel was made a trusted leader in Babylon. Other leaders became jealous and passed a law for the purpose of getting rid of Daniel. These same men turned Daniel in when he disobeyed it. Sentenced to death, Daniel was thrown into the lion's den. However, God spared him from the lions and Daniel emerged unharmed the next day. Because of the wonders he had seen, King Darius praised the God of Daniel. He also sent a decree to all peoples and men of every language that they must fear and revere the God of Daniel. God's name spread. God blessed Daniel out of of love and also in light of His purpose to be known in every nation!

BEGIN BY READING WITH YOUR FAMILY:

Daniel 6:3-28

FAMILY ACTIVITY

Teaching Time: 10 minutes
Materials: Daniel cutout (optional), ball, wall

Find a wall inside or outside of your house to bounce the ball against. Have family members line up side-by-side, facing the wall. Explain that the ball represents God's blessing. Throw the ball at the wall. When it bounces off, the next person in line should catch it. God first blessed Daniel by rescuing him from the lions. Invite "Daniel" to bounce the ball off the wall for the next person to catch. Next God's blessing was passed to King Darius who learned about the true God. Invite "King Darius" to bounce the ball off the wall for the next person to catch. Then God's blessing extended to all peoples in the kingdom. King Darius wrote to them telling them of the God of Daniel. Repeat the activity as many times as you want. Have your children state how God's blessing was passed on as they throw the ball towards the wall or catch it.

DISCUSS

1. What three people or groups of people were blessed by God? How did God bless them? What was the greater purpose of God's blessing Daniel?

2. King Darius learned about God by watching Daniel. What can others around you learn about God by watching your family?

PRAY

Pray that God would use your family to demonstrate who God is to others.

24 Future of Nations Foretold
THE PROPHETS

As we go deeper into the Old Testament, we see the nation of Israel become more and more disobedient. God raised up both major and minor prophets to remind Israel of their calling to be a holy, set-apart people who reflected Him to the surrounding nations. These prophets called Israel to repent and tried to steer the nation back on course. Although some of the prophetic writings focus on Israel, God has not forgotten about the Gentiles (non-Jewish nations). Many prophecies reveal much about God's future plans for the nations.

BEGIN BY READING WITH YOUR FAMILY:

Isaiah 12:4-6; Zechariah 2:10-11, 8:20-23; Malachi 1:11

 FAMILY ACTIVITY

Teaching Time: 10 minutes
Materials: The Prophets cutout (optional), outside space

Point out the place where the sun rises and sets in your neighborhood. Explain that God's name will be great from one end of the world to the other and everywhere in between. Discuss what it might look like for believers to shout for joy and tell the nations what God has done. Ask your family if they think they can shout loudly enough for the whole world to hear—from where the sun rises to where it sets. Hold a contest to see who can shout the loudest. Have the first person turn towards where the sun rises and shout "God is great!" Then direct him to shout "God is great!" in the direction the sun sets, as if shouting to the whole world. The next person should try to shout it louder, and so on.

 DISCUSS

1. Why would God want us to speak of what He has done?

2. Since we are not able to shout loud enough for the whole world to hear us, how do you think God could use our family to tell the world of what He has done?

 PRAY

Pray that the world would hear of all that God has done.

NEW TESTAMENT

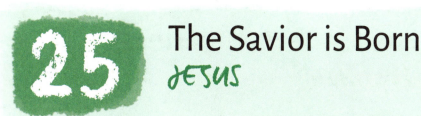

25 The Savior is Born
JESUS

Separating the Old and New Testament writings are 400 years with no recorded words from the Lord. God was still silently at work, orchestrating historical events to prepare the world for the arrival of Jesus. After Jesus was born, Jewish shepherds and Gentile wise men came to worship Him. Following Jewish custom, Jesus' parents presented him at the temple shortly after His birth. Simeon was there, awaiting the fulfillment of God's promise that before his death, he would see the Messiah with his own eyes. Holding baby Jesus in his arms, Simeon proclaimed, "For my eyes have seen your salvation which you have prepared in the sight of all people, a light for revelation to the Gentiles and the glory of your people Israel" (Luke 2:30-32). Jesus' primary mission was announced as His parents looked on with wonder.

BEGIN BY READING WITH YOUR FAMILY:

Luke 2:4-33

FAMILY ACTIVITY

Teaching Time: 15 minutes
Materials: Jesus child-sized cutout (optional); Bible; timer (optional); towel, cloth, or small mat; piece of string or yarn longer than your cloth

Hold up your Bible and invite your children to put one finger on the section separating the Old and New Testaments. Share that 400 years passed between the time of Malachi and Matthew. We have no record of God's speaking to His people during that time. Simulate this period of silence by setting a timer for 40 seconds (or have an adult count slowly and silently to 40). Put your hands over your mouths and stay quiet until the timer goes off (or parent who is counting calls time). Invite a child to stretch out the string under the towel so that the ends stick out on either side. Point to one end of the string and explain that in the Old Testament, God promised to bless the nations through Abraham's family. Trace the path of the string running beneath the towel. Even though God's actions were hidden from people for 400 years, He was preparing events in history to bring about that blessing. Point to the other end of the string. As the New Testament began, God started to speak to His people again, including Mary, Joseph, the shepherds, the wise men, and Simeon. God's promised blessing had finally arrived. Discuss who that person was. Shout, "Jesus" together.

DISCUSS

1. Look at Luke 2:11 and 2:30-32. To whom was Jesus sent? How would Jesus become a blessing to them?

2. God's promise to bless the nations continues today and He invites believers to join with Him. Write your family's last name/surname on a sticky note and attach it near the end of the string. Read 1 Peter 3:15. How can our family be a blessing to those who do not yet know Jesus?

PRAY

Ask God for to give your family opportunities to share Jesus with those who do not yet know Him.

About His Father's Business
JESUS' CHILDHOOD

Jesus grew up in the small village of Nazareth (Matthew 2:22-23). His earthly father was a carpenter who provided for their family, including Jesus' younger brothers and sisters (Matthew 13:55). Jesus developed like other children. He got taller and stronger. He learned to think and make wise decisions. He learned how to obey His parents and make friends. Most importantly, Jesus learned to love God. At age twelve, Jesus traveled to Jerusalem with His family for the Feast of Passover. Afterwards, Jesus remained behind. After three days of searching, his parents found Jesus in the temple, listening to the teachers and asking questions. Jesus asked, "Why did you seek Me? Did you not know that I must be about My Father's business?" (Luke 2:49, NKJV) Although Jesus returned home and remained obedient to His parents, He recognized that His relationship to His heavenly father, and devotion to God's purposes for His life, took top priority.

BEGIN BY READING WITH YOUR FAMILY:

Luke 2:40-52

FAMILY ACTIVITY

Teaching Time: 15 minutes
Materials: Jesus child-sized cutout (optional); paper, pen or pencil; markers or crayons

Explain to your children that Jesus did not begin his life on earth as an adult, but was born as a baby and grew in many of the ways they do. Help your children make a booklet comparing their childhood and Jesus' childhood. Write and illustrate statements such as:

- Jesus had brothers and sisters. I have _____.
- Jesus' parent was a carpenter. My parent is _____.
- Jesus lived in the town of Nazareth. I live in _____.
- Jesus learned about God by _____. I learn about God by _____.

DISCUSS

1. How are you similar to Jesus? How are you different?
2. What was "my Father's business" in Jesus' day? What is being about our Father's business today?

PRAY

Pray that your family would be about your heavenly Father's business and ask Him what that looks like for your family.

 # A Jewish Rejection
JESUS' PUBLIC READING

Jesus stood in His hometown synagogue and unrolled a scroll. Reading from Isaiah 61, Jesus proclaimed His purpose: to preach good news to the poor, recover sight to the blind, and release the oppressed. Everyone spoke well of Him until Jesus pointed out their past rejection of God and questioned their privileged status as God's chosen people. Jesus referenced two instances where God rescued Gentiles, despite the many Jewish people suffering at the same time. During a famine, God sent Elijah to a Gentile widow (1 Kings 17). God sent Elisha to heal Naaman, an uncircumcised commander of the Syrian army (2 Kings 5)! These references infuriated the Jewish listeners. They wanted the Messiah to come and rescue them only, no one else. In their anger, they tried to seize Jesus and throw Him off a cliff! Jesus miraculously got away. Jesus was making a clear opening statement about His ministry and life. Although He was still about fulfilling His promises to Abraham and would focus a great deal on the lost sheep of Israel, Jesus ultimately would become Savior of the world (for Jew, Greek and Gentile).

BEGIN BY READING WITH YOUR FAMILY:

Luke 4:14-30

 **FAMILY ACTIVITY**

Teaching Time: 10 minutes
Materials: Jesus adult-sized cutout (optional), two pages from a coloring book or two pieces of drawing paper, box of crayons

Place one coloring sheet in front of your children. Invite them to take turns coloring a picture using only one crayon color. Discuss how the Jewish people thought the Messiah was coming to save them only. Then lay out the second coloring sheet. Invite your children to use every color in the crayon box to complete a picture. Discuss how Jesus would be a Messiah who would save people of all nations.

 DISCUSS

1. Read Revelation 7:9. Based on this verse, how many people groups will be in heaven - a few, some, every group? Which coloring sheet more accurately represents what heaven will be like?

2. If using all the colors in the crayon box creates a more complete picture, why do you think God wants to include people from every tribe, tongue, and nation in His kingdom?

 PRAY

Read God's promise in Psalm 86:9 and pray that all nations will come and worship before the Lord.

 Fishers of Men
JESUS' DISCIPLES

Jesus called twelve disciples. He spent three years with this small band of men who would someday be fishers of other men. This was part of His strategy. Jesus was not concerned about programs that might reach the multitudes. Instead, He focused on investing in the men whom the multitudes would one day follow and learn from. In the future, these same men would take over Jesus' work and spread the gospel far and wide.

BEGIN BY READING WITH YOUR FAMILY:

Luke 5:1-11

 FAMILY ACTIVITY

Teaching Time: 10 minutes
Materials: Jesus and The Disciples cutouts (optional)

Announce that you will do a series of crazy motions and invite your family to copy you exactly. Then go into an adjoining room where you cannot be seen to do the motions. Ask if family members copied your actions and discuss the problem of their being unable to see you. Choose one child to return with you to the adjoining room. Position him where he can see you and also be seen by the rest of the family. As you do each motion, have the child observe you and then demonstrate it for the others to copy. Why was the task easier to complete the second time? Explain that Jesus chose twelve disciples who observed His actions, listened to His teaching, and helped in ministry. Jesus trained them and gave them the authority to teach others. Share that after Jesus returned to heaven, people would no longer be able to see and hear Jesus, but they would come to know Jesus by observing how His disciples lived and listening to their teaching. Jesus' disciples had imitated Him. Now others would imitate them.

 DISCUSS

1. What does it mean to be fishers of men? What does this look like in everyday life?

2. Read 1 Corinthians 11:1. Paul invites people who want to live like Jesus to follow his (Paul's) example. How can our family be an example of Jesus for others to imitate?

 PRAY

Ask God to connect you with another family that you can begin to disciple.

# A Confused Teacher Redirected
NICODEMUS

Nicodemus, a Jewish leader, came to Jesus in the dark of night. He was confused and wanted to talk to the teacher who had come from God. Nicodemus and Jesus talked about being born again of the Spirit. Then Jesus uttered some of the most quoted words in history: "For God so loved the world, that he gave his one and only son..." (John 3:16). Jesus continued to clarify who He was and what He had been sent to do. He had come to bring salvation not only to the Jewish nation, but to all peoples.

BEGIN BY READING WITH YOUR FAMILY:

John 3:1-17

 FAMILY ACTIVITY

Teaching Time: 10 minutes
Materials: Nicodemus cutout (optional), world map, Bible

Explain that Jesus came to die for the sins of people in every culture and bring new life to those who believe in Him. Spread the world map on the floor. Choose one child to close his eyes and move his finger slowly across the map. Have someone else say "stop" at a random time. Upon hearing "stop", have your child freeze his finger's position, open his eyes, and look at the country his finger is touching (or nearest to if he is touching water). Recite John 3:16 and include that country like this: "For God so loved _ [country name] that He gave His one and only Son, that whoever believes in Him shall not perish but have eternal life." Take turns tracing your finger over the map and quoting the verse for different countries. After a few turns, say John 3:16 together as a family.

 DISCUSS

1. What is God's desire and plan for the unreached peoples of the world?
2. Read John 14:6. There are many other religions that people around the world follow. What does this verse say happens to people who do not follow Jesus?

 PRAY

Pray that unreached peoples will come to know the God who loves them and sent His Son Jesus to die for their sins.

30 Encountering the Savior of the World
THE SAMARITAN WOMAN

While traveling through Samaria with His disciples, Jesus encountered a Samaritan woman fetching water at the village well. Despised because of her race, this woman had little value in most people's eyes. Yet, Jesus sought her out, offered her living water that would satisfy her deepest need, and explained that He was the Messiah. After the woman shared about her encounter with Jesus, curious villagers set off to see Jesus for themselves. Knowing that Samaritans were coming to meet Him at that very moment, Jesus told His disciples, "I tell you, open your eyes and look at the fields! They are ripe for harvest" (John 4:35). Because of this woman's testimony and Jesus' own words, many Samaritans believed. These despised people were the first to acknowledge Jesus as the Savior of the world. This account demonstrates God's intense love for individuals and how He used that love to bring an entire people to Himself.

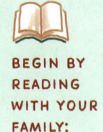

BEGIN BY READING WITH YOUR FAMILY:

John 4:4-35, 39-42

FAMILY ACTIVITY

Teaching Time: 10 minutes
Materials: Samaritan Woman cutout (optional); water in a sink, tub, bucket, or pond; rock

Look at the water and describe the surface. The still water is like the Samaritan village before Jesus visited. Now talk about what happened when first Jesus entered the village. Explain that Jesus chose to share His message of salvation with one person and discuss who that individual was. Then take turns dropping the rock into the water. Observe and count the rings of ripples created by only one rock. Share with your children how Jesus' message affected the Samaritan woman in a powerful way. The impact of Jesus' message did not stop with her, but rippled out to others. Talk about others who heard about Jesus through the woman's testimony and how they responded.

DISCUSS

1. God's Son, Jesus, chose to speak to a person who was despised and ignored. What does this demonstrate about God? Read Romans 5:8. How is each of us like the Samaritan woman?

2. God gave the Samaritan woman the privilege of being the first person in the entire village to know the Savior of the world. What was God's greater purpose for this blessing?

PRAY

Pray for people who have never had the opportunity to hear that Jesus is the Savior of the world.

Jesus Heals Gentiles
CENTURION'S SERVANT

Jesus spent much of His ministry fulfilling Isaiah's prophecy about what the coming Messiah would do. He preached good news to the poor, proclaimed freedom for the prisoners, recovered the sight of the blind, and set the oppressed free (Isaiah 61:1). It is amazing that many of the miracles recorded in the gospels were not for the Jewish people, but for Gentiles! One example is the healing of a Roman centurion's servant. Jesus praised the faith of this army commander, saying He had not found anyone with such great faith in all of Israel. Jesus challenged the Jews' assumption that God's messiah was only for them by saying, "… many will come from the east and the west, and will take their places at the feast with Abraham, Isaac, and Jacob in the kingdom of heaven" (Matthew 8:11).

BEGIN BY READING WITH YOUR FAMILY:
Matthew 8:5-13

FAMILY ACTIVITY

Teaching Time: 12 minutes
Materials: Jesus cutout (optional), one 61 cm (24 in) piece of string or yarn, two 20 cm (8 in) pieces of string or yarn

Invite your children to tie a knot in the long string for each Old or New Testament Israelite that they can name. These Israelites were people in the family line of Abraham. They thought the promised Messiah would come to save them only. Discuss the healing of the Roman centurion's servant. Why did Jesus honor this army commander's request? Invite a child to tie a knot in one of the short strings. Read Matthew 8:11 and explain that the two shorter strings stand for the Gentiles from the east and west who, like the centurion, would put their faith in Jesus. Have the children tie the shorter strings to both sides of the longer string to form the shape of a cross. Explain how Jesus' death on the cross makes a way for all peoples to have a relationship with God.

DISCUSS

1. Read Matthew 8:10. How did the centurion amaze Jesus? Is faith limited to people of certain regions, cultures, or backgrounds?

2. Name some people groups who have not heard about Jesus yet. Insert their name into Jesus' promise in Matthew 8:11: "___ will take their places at the feast with Abraham, Isaac, and Jacob in the kingdom of heaven." How can our family help unreached peoples take their place in God's heavenly kingdom?

PRAY

Pray that unreached peoples from east, west, north, and south will come to know and follow Jesus.

 Jesus Heals Gentiles
DEMON-POSSESSED MAN

Jesus took His disciples to the region of the Gerasenes where many Gentiles lived. There, they encountered a demon-possessed man living among the tombs, isolated from his family and community. Multiple demons caused him to fly into uncontrollable rages and injure himself. Jesus cast out the demons, leaving the man calm and in his right mind. Longing to follow Jesus, the man begged to journey with Him. But Jesus said, "Go home to your own people and tell them how much the Lord has done for you, and how he has had mercy on you" (Mark 5:19). Jesus did not heal this man because of his race or religious background, but out of mercy. Jesus desired for this story of God's mercy to spread to other Gentiles-the family, friends, and local community of the healed man.

BEGIN BY READING WITH YOUR FAMILY:

Mark 5:1-20

 FAMILY ACTIVITY

Teaching Time: 15 minutes
Materials: Jesus cutout (optional); paper for drawing; crayons, colored pencils, or markers

Give each child a piece of drawing paper. Have them fold the paper in half to make two columns. Label one column "Without Jesus" and the other column "With Jesus". As a family, discuss how the demon-possessed man changed after Jesus healed him. Include ideas about where he lived, how he dressed, how he behaved, how he demonstrated his emotions, and how he interacted with other people. Invite your children to draw before and after pictures of the man and his surroundings. Use their pictures to talk about the complete transformation that Jesus brings. Read Mark 5:18-20 and use the verses to discuss why Jesus refused to let the healed man join Him. Explain how Jesus' plan for the healed man demonstrated God's mercy.

 DISCUSS

1. Do we know people whose lives have been transformed by Jesus? How have they changed?

2. God used the healed man to bring the gospel to other Gentiles, starting with people he knew best. When a person from an unreached culture trusts in Jesus today, how might God use this same plan?

 PRAY

Pray that unreached people who come to know Jesus will be bold in sharing what God has done for them with their family, friends, teachers, co-workers, and neighbors.

33 Jesus' Sending Strategy
THE TWELVE AND THE SEVENTY

Jesus' ministry plan was strategic. Knowing that God had prepared Israelites to understand the gospel, Jesus first expended significant effort to reach them and form His Jewish following. He revealed this part of God's plan by sending His twelve disciples to the "lost sheep of the house of Israel." Later Jesus revealed more of God's plan by sending seventy others to "every city and place to which He Himself was going to come." This included regions where Gentiles were prevalent. Seventy was an important number for Jews. One thing it brought to their minds was the number of nations, or peoples, who descended from Noah (Genesis 10). Through His actions, Jesus may have foreshadowed His future commissioning of believers to make disciples of all nations (Matthew 28:19).

BEGIN BY READING WITH YOUR FAMILY:

Matthew 10:1-8; Luke 10:1

FAMILY ACTIVITY

Teaching Time: 15 minutes
Materials: Jesus cutout (optional), paper, crayons or colored pencils, scissors

Have each child draw a picture that covers his entire piece of paper, and make sure that no one else sees it. Have a parent collect the pictures and roll them up so that the picture is hidden on the inside. Take turns unrolling the pictures a little at a time, stopping to make guesses about what the picture is. Read Matthew 10:5 together and ask who would hear the gospel first. Then, read Luke 10:1 to find out where Jesus sent His followers next. Refer back to the rolled up pictures and explain that God always planned to reach the whole world with the gospel, but He revealed His plan a little at a time.

DISCUSS

1. God blessed the nation of Israel by revealing Himself to them first. What did God want Israel to do with this blessing?
2. We have been blessed with a relationship with the true God. What does God want our family to do with this blessing?

PRAY

Pray that God will give your family a heart for people around the world who are still waiting for the gospel to reach them.

Jesus' Double Miracle
FEEDING 5,000 AND 4,000

After feeding 5,000 hungry Jews in Galilee with just five loaves and two fish, the disciples faced a similar situation some months later. This time they encountered 4,000 hungry Gentiles in the Decapolis, a region inhabited by Greeks and other foreigners (Mark 7:31). If Jesus performed a feeding miracle here, it would demonstrate that He was willing to do the same kind of miracle for the Gentiles as He had done for the Jews. Through this act, Jesus continued to expand His disciples' paradigm, wanting them to understand His compassion and desire for all peoples to know Him as Lord.

BEGIN BY READING WITH YOUR FAMILY:

Matthew 15:29-39

FAMILY ACTIVITY

Teaching Time: 15 minutes
Materials: Jesus cutout (optional), paper, pen or marker, string that is 10 cm (4 in) long

Setting Up: Before gathering your family, prepare this optical illusion. On your paper, draw a straight, horizontal line segment about 10 cm (4 in) long. About 5 cm (2 in) below this line, draw a second parallel line segment of the same length. Add short, slanted lines to the ends of each line segment like this:

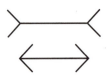

Show your family the two line drawings. Take turns guessing which middle line segment is longer. Afterwards, announce that both lines are exactly the same length. Invite your children to lay the string on top of each line segment for proof. Discuss what is different about the two drawings. Explain that the shapes surrounding each line segment make them appear to be different lengths. Connect this activity to the similar situations the disciples faced. Both crowds were hungry and Jesus had the power to miraculously feed both groups. However, the first crowd had been Jewish, but this hungry crowd was Gentile. Discuss differences between Jews and Gentiles and explain why the disciples may have doubted that Jesus would choose to do a miraculous feeding this time. Think through what Jesus demonstrated to His disciples when He invited them to help Him feed 4,000 Gentiles.

DISCUSS

1. The disciples focused on the differences between Jews and Gentiles. Read Romans 3:22-24. In God's eyes, how are Jews and Gentiles the same?

2. What people in our world today are often considered outside the reach of Jesus' compassion and salvation?

PRAY

Pray that God will help your family view other people through His eyes.

A Shepherd's Flock
OTHER SHEEP

The Pharisees, the leaders and guardians of Israel, banished a former blind man from the synagogue (John 9:34). What was his offence? This Jewish man had testified of Jesus' healing and divine nature. Jesus began to challenge the Pharisees, using parables about sheep, thieves, and true shepherds. Jesus made it clear that the sheepfold is the nation of Israel (John 10:16). Jesus is the door of the sheepfold and makes it possible for the sheep to leave the fold (Judaism) and to enter His flock. The Pharisees expelled the healed man from the synagogue, but Jesus led him out of Judaism and into the flock of God. Jesus went on to talk about sheep "not of this fold"—Gentile followers. In His early ministry, Jesus focused on the "lost sheep of Israel" (Matthew 10:5-6), but the Church was not to remain a "Jewish flock." There is but one flock, the people of God who belong to the Good Shepherd, and He will call them and gather them together.

BEGIN BY READING WITH YOUR FAMILY:

John 10:7-18

FAMILY ACTIVITY

Teaching Time: 15 minutes
Materials: Jesus cutout (optional); 12 small, similar items to represent sheep (coins, rocks, buttons, beads, blocks, etc.); two chairs or cushions

Let your children place six "sheep" on the seat of a chair or cushion to represent the the people of Israel who were waiting for the promised Messiah to come. Let children scatter the remaining "sheep" around the house. Point to the "Israelite sheep" on the chair and explain that many Jews did not believe Jesus was the promised Savior. But whenever Jews recognized and followed Jesus as their Messiah, He invited them to leave their pen and become part of a new flock that He was creating. Let each child take an "Israelite sheep" and move it to the other chair to demonstrate this new flock. Explain that God always planned for this new flock to include Gentile people from all around the world. Send your children to retrieve a scattered "sheep" and add it to the new flock. Discuss how the sheep in the new flock are neither Jews nor Gentiles, but believers in Jesus.

DISCUSS

1. What makes Jesus such a great shepherd? How do people become a part of Jesus' flock?
2. Have your children show you where they scattered the remaining objects. Are there people from other cultures and religions who are scattered throughout our city or region? Why do you think God has placed them here?

PRAY

Ask God to connect your family to someone from another culture or religion who has never had the opportunity to hear about the Good Shepherd.

# Promise of the Church
PETER

Jesus took His disciples into a Gentile region strongly identified with pagan religions. A former center of Baal worship, Caesarea Philippi had multiple shrines to Greek gods and a gleaming Roman temple built to honor Caesar. Surrounded by false gods, Peter first confessed that Jesus was the Son of God. In response, Jesus announced, "I will build My church." To the disciples, "church" meant small assemblies of Israelite worshipers. Jesus was expanding their paradigm. Jesus would unite believing Jews and Gentiles, bringing them together as a new assembly, where there were no distinctions. Peter would be a part of unleashing this new assembly. It would not be built on him (petros-a stone), but on Jesus (petra-a large rock). Peter would join with God in opening "the door of faith" to the Jews at Pentecost (Acts 2), to the Samaritans (Acts 8:14), and to the Gentiles (Acts 10).

BEGIN BY READING WITH YOUR FAMILY:

Matthew 16:13-20

 FAMILY ACTIVITY

Teaching Time: 15 minutes
Materials: Jesus and Peter cutouts (optional)

Beforehand, open all of the doors in your house, including the closets and cabinets. Then invite your family to meet by one door. Explain how the nation of Israel believed that the doors to God's love and mercy were closed to everyone but them, and ask children to go around the house closing every open door that they see. Share that when Jesus announced that He would build His church, He was announcing open access to God for all peoples. Open a door and explain that God welcomes the Jews. Then open another door. God also welcomes the Samaritans. Finally, have everyone go around the house and open all doors. Explain how God welcomes all Gentile nations. Jesus' church is not a place, but people from all nations and time periods who have come to God through trusting Jesus as their Savior.

 DISCUSS

1. What individuals or cultures is our family shutting out of God's family in our hearts and minds? Why do we believe they are outside of God's grace?

2. Who builds and watches over the Church? (see Matthew 16:18) How should this encourage us as we share the gospel with others?

 PRAY

Pray that God will help your family view the peoples of the world as potential members of God's global Church.

 # God's Temple Misused
JESUS CLEARS THE COURTS

Jesus and His disciples came to Jerusalem. Because of the upcoming Passover observance, people from all over Israel, as well as Gentile seekers, filled the city. Entering the temple, Jesus found that the outer courts reserved for Gentiles were crowded with Jewish money changers and sellers. In a display of righteous anger, Jesus began flipping over their tables. He scolded them, saying they had turned the temple into a den of robbers when it was intended to be a house of prayer for all nations. Israel had turned their blessing inward, taking advantage of God's house for their own benefit.

BEGIN BY READING WITH YOUR FAMILY:
Mark 11:15-18; 1 Kings 8:41-43

 ### FAMILY ACTIVITY

Teaching Time: 15 minutes
Materials: Jesus cutout (optional); a cup; dirt, rocks, or sand; picture of a church

Work together to think of the most common ways that people use cups. Now take the cup outside and invite your children to fill it with dirt, rocks, or sand. Talk about the possibility of planting a flower in the cup. Think through the ramifications for thirsty people if your family decided to plant flowers in every cup in your home. Problems would arise when cups were not used for their primary purpose. Now talk about the main purpose for the temple in Jesus' day. What problems were the Jewish money changers and sellers causing for the people coming into the outer courts of the temple? Discuss how their actions were an obstacle to worship.

 ### DISCUSS

1. What was God's initial plan for the temple when it was built in Solomon's day? How did God intend to use it to make His name known among the nations?

2. Read Mark 11:17. How did the money changers go against God's plan? How can our local church be a house of prayer for all nations?

 ### PRAY

With the picture of the church in front of you, pray that your local church will become a place where prayers are offered for unreached peoples.

 # Greeks Seeking a Visit
JESUS PREDICTS HIS DEATH

Near the end of Jesus' earthly ministry, He faced mixed reactions. Crowds cheered during His triumphal entry into Jerusalem, children praised Him in the temple, and many Jewish leaders sought His death. Visiting Greeks heard about Jesus and desired to meet with Him. When Philip and Andrew delivered their request, Jesus' response was unexpected. It was neither, "Let them come" nor "Send them away." Instead Jesus replied, "The hour has come for the Son of Man to be glorified." The deep interest of the Greeks in seeing Jesus was evidence that the world was now fully ready for the culmination of His redemptive plan for all peoples—His death on the cross. When He had been lifted up from the earth, Jesus would draw all men, both Jews and Gentiles, to Himself (John 12:32).

BEGIN BY READING WITH YOUR FAMILY:
John 12:20-36

 ## FAMILY ACTIVITY

Teaching Time: 8 minutes
Materials: Jesus cutout (optional); two sticks or drawing paper, crayons, and markers; 6-8 small pieces of paper; pencil or pen; string, scissors, tape

Work together to create a cross. You can either fasten two sticks together with string or draw a picture of a cross and tape the picture down so it will not move. Write "Jew" on one small piece of paper and "Gentile" on another piece. On the remaining pieces, write the names of unreached people groups or lost people that you know. Cut 6-8 pieces of string, each about half a meter (2 ft) in length. Tape one end of each string to one of your small pieces of paper. Tie or tape the other ends of the strings to the cross. Take turns pulling each string towards the cross. Say, "Jesus will draw __ (insert words on the paper) to Himself."

 ## DISCUSS

1. How would Jesus be lifted up from the earth in His death? Why is Jesus' death on the cross important to my salvation?

2. Read Luke 24:46-47. How far does Jesus' forgiveness extend? Why is it so important for us to share the good news of Jesus with unreached peoples?

 ## PRAY

Pray that all nations will have the opportunity to hear the truth of Jesus.

 A Debt is Paid
JESUS' DEATH AND RESURRECTION

Jesus spent the days leading up to His crucifixion with His disciples, preparing them for what was ahead. Jesus was arrested, questioned, and passed along to different rulers. All the while the Jews cried, "Crucify Him!" Hanging on the cross between two thieves, Jesus declared the type of Savior He was. He offered the confessing thief forgiveness and promised that he would be with Jesus in paradise that very day. After Jesus' death, the temple veil which prevented humans from coming into the presence of God, was torn in half. Jesus was buried in a tomb, but three days later, it was empty. God's promise to Abraham, to bless all families of the earth, was partially fulfilled by Jesus' death and resurrection. Jesus appeared to Mary Magdalene and she became the first evangelist, telling others of the risen Lord. Jesus spent 40 days with His disciples, teaching them all that the Scriptures had said about Him.

BEGIN BY READING WITH YOUR FAMILY:

Luke 23:13-25, 32-46; Matthew 27:57-61; Mark 16:1-7

 FAMILY ACTIVITY

Teaching Time: 10 minutes
Materials: Jesus cutout (optional); two points near your home, with one point being higher than the other (a staircase, steps, ramp, hill); Bible marked at Psalm 40:11-13

Have your children stand at the low point while you stand at the higher. Tell your children that their position is dangerous, but they can be saved if they can get to where you are. While remaining where they are, have your children discuss different ways they might reach you. They must ask you if they can use a suggested plan before attempting it. Refuse all ideas that involve their working to get to you. After several ideas are discussed, lead your children to discover that the only way they can be rescued is for you to come and get them. Give younger children a hint like, "You cannot come to me, but I can come ___." They must complete the rest of the sentence. Give older children the Bible marked at Psalm 40:11-13. Invite them to read the passage and apply it to their situation. When your children ask if you can come and bring them to your location, wholeheartedly agree!

 DISCUSS

1. Read Romans 3:23. What separates us from God? What did Jesus do to bring us to God and rescue us from the danger of sin?

2. Many people in our world have never heard about Jesus. How might they try to approach God on their own. Read John 14:6. What is the only way we can have a relationship with God? What are some things our family can do so that these people learn about the only way to God?

 PRAY

Thank God for providing Jesus. Ask God to show your family ways to be involved in helping others find the only way to God.

The Great Commission
JESUS' LAST WORDS

Jesus' Great Commission was not a new concept He taught minutes before ascending into heaven, but rather the crescendo of all He was showing His people. Jesus had emphasized the global scale of God's heart and plan throughout His ministry. Not confined to Matthew 28, the Great Commission is found in all four gospels, as well as Acts. As God sent Jesus into the world, so Jesus is sending us (John 20:21). He promises to be with us always as we go out in obedience to make disciples of all nations. Jesus was not referring to countries, but to ethnic people groups, each with a unique culture. Although Jesus commanded us to make disciples in every people group, more than one-third of today's people groups do not have access to the gospel.

BEGIN BY READING WITH YOUR FAMILY:

Matthew 28:18-20; Mark 16:15; Luke 24:45-47; John 20:21; Acts 1:8

FAMILY ACTIVITY

Teaching Time: 10 minutes
Materials: Jesus cutout (optional)

As a family, make up a simple clapping pattern. Practice until everyone can do it easily. Invite one person to clap the pattern alone. Next have two people clap the pattern together. Now add a third person. Finally have the whole family clap the pattern together. Explain that although different people participated in clapping, the pattern sounded the same except that the volume increased with each repetition. Read Matthew 28:16-20 and share that these were Jesus's last words to His followers before returning to heaven. Rather than giving new instructions, Jesus was repeating a command He had already given to His followers many times. Jesus had often spoken about making disciples of all nations, using slightly different words. Believers often refer to this command as the "Great Commission."

Option: For small families, one person can take two turns by clapping the pattern on one knee, then on both knees the second time.

DISCUSS

1. What are some phrases or instructions that parents or teachers repeat often? How does repetition help us? (To learn, to remember, to know what is most important). What does Jesus' repetition of the Great Commission reflect about God's heart for the world?

2. Have all the people around the world heard about Jesus? How can our family be obedient to the Great Commission of Jesus?

PRAY

Choose one place or culture where the gospel has not yet reached. Pray for the good news of Jesus to be proclaimed there.

41 Outpouring of God's Spirit
PENTECOST

After Jesus' death, Jerusalem was a dangerous place for His followers (Acts 1:11), but it was also a strategic city. God chose to coordinate the outpouring of His Spirit with an annual Jewish festival centered in Jerusalem. As the disciples waited obediently for the gift of the Holy Spirit, God was bringing to Jerusalem Jews "from every nation under Heaven" (Acts 2:5). After being filled with the Holy Spirit, Peter and the disciples testified about Jesus before a huge crowd-- in words that men of every language could understand. In that moment, the disciples boldly began to fulfill Jesus' command to be witnesses in Jerusalem. Three thousand people believed that the resurrected Jesus was their Savior. These new believers began to meet together for fellowship, teaching, prayer, and mutual care. God began to establish an unshakeable, worldwide Church!

BEGIN BY READING WITH YOUR FAMILY:

Acts 2:1-14, 22-24, 36-41

FAMILY ACTIVITY

Teaching Time: 15 minutes
Materials: The Disciples cutout (optional), world map, string, scissors

Gather around a world map on the floor or a table. Invite a child to locate the country of Israel. Explain that after the coming of the Holy Spirit in Jerusalem, the gospel message began to spread from that area to other parts of the world. Use history to discuss people who may have brought the gospel to the country where you live. Now chart the gospel's route using pieces of string cut to the correct length. First connect Israel to the country of those who brought the gospel to your people. Then use a second piece of string to connect that country to your home country. Think about believers you know who have taken the gospel from your country to other parts of the world. Use more string to connect your home country to the places you discuss. While looking at all the strings, explain that by God's power, believers have taken the gospel message to many parts of the world. As people in these places put their trust in Jesus, they become part of the worldwide Church.

DISCUSS

1. How did believers travel with the gospel in the early church? Discuss transportation in Bible times. How do believers spread the gospel to new areas today? Discuss modern transportation and technology.

2. Who brought the gospel to our family? Discuss specific people. How can our family participate in spreading of the gospel to new areas?

PRAY

Cut a small piece of string for each family member to hold. Ask God to use your family to spread the gospel from your home to the nations.

 # Purposeful Persecution
BELIEVERS SCATTERED

After making disciples in the city of Jerusalem, the regions of Judea and Samaria were next. However, the believers had settled in Jerusalem. Who would go and how would they get there? God had a plan. Following the stoning death of Stephen, great persecution broke out against the believers in Jerusalem. Although the apostles stayed in Jerusalem where they were most strategic to the cause of Christ, the rest of the believers fled throughout Judea and Samaria. Those who were scattered preached the word wherever they went. God used persecution to spread believers to the next regions. From there, the witness of Jesus continued to spread throughout the land, but no longer to the Jews only.

BEGIN BY READING WITH YOUR FAMILY:

Acts 6:7-14; 7:51-60; 8:1-4

 ## FAMILY ACTIVITY

Teaching Time: 15 minutes
Materials: Persecuted Believers cutout (optional), light-weight sturdy objects (blocks, legos, small boxes, empty soda cans or bottles), apple or ball

Go outside to an open area. Have your children pile or stack the objects. Stand about 2.5-3 m (8-10 ft) away. Take turns throwing the apple or ball at the pile. Restack objects as needed. Observe what happens to the objects when they get hit. See who can scatter the objects the furthest. Explain that just like the pile of objects, the first believers in the early church stayed together all in one place--the city of Jerusalem. What caused the believers to scatter into new areas?

 ## DISCUSS

1. Have you ever moved to or visited a new place? What things did you take with you? Read Acts 8:4. What important thing did the persecuted believers take with them when they scattered? How did this further the Great Commission of Jesus?

2. Have you or anyone you know been persecuted because of his faith in Jesus? How? How might God use modern-day persecution to make His name known to unbelievers?

 ## PRAY

Choose one country where believers face persecution for their faith in Jesus. Pray that God will fill them with courage and hope.

# 43 Samaritans Receive the Spirit
Philip

Many believers spread out from Jerusalem, including Philip, a deacon in the early church (Acts 6:5). Philip went to a city in Samaria and proclaimed Jesus to the Samaritans, a people whose lineage was half Jew, half Gentile. This was the first cross-cultural movement of the gospel. When the Samaritans believed in Jesus, Philip baptized them. When apostles in Jerusalem heard this news, they sent Peter and John to the city where Philip was. Although the Samaritans had put their faith in Jesus and been baptized, they did not yet have the Holy Spirit. When Peter and John arrived, they laid hands on these new believers and prayed for them to receive God's Spirit. The Holy Spirit came upon them, demonstrating that God was working among the Samaritans as well as among the Jews.

BEGIN BY READING WITH YOUR FAMILY:

Acts 8:5-25

 ## FAMILY ACTIVITY

Teaching Time: 15 minutes
Materials: Philip cutout (optional); piece of string 60 cm (2 ft) long; tape; 2 cups of similar size; water; outside area, sink, bathtub, or protected surface

Practice this water activity until you can do it easily for your family.

Soak the string in water. Then invite your child to tape one end of it to the bottom inside of an empty cup. Fill the other cup halfway with water, and hold the other end of the string inside the rim of it with your index finger. Lift the full cup higher than the empty cup to stretch the string until it is taut. After you do this, explain that the water represents the gospel in Jewish regions, the string is like the Holy Spirit who has the power to transform the hearts of all who put their faith in Jesus, and the empty cup is like the Samaritan region. Then tilt the top cup at a 45-degree angle and slowly begin pouring the water down the string. Water should travel down the string and fill the empty cup. As your children watch, share how God used the Holy Spirit not only to to take the gospel to the Samaritans, but also to teach the apostles that there was no culture He could not enter.

 ## DISCUSS

1. How does this biblical account show that the gospel is not limited to one region or group of people?

2. How did Philip join with God in advancing the gospel? (see Acts 8:5, 12) How can our family join with God in advancing the gospel among unreached peoples today?

 ## PRAY

Pray that God will give your family creative ways to partner with goers (cross-cultural workers) who bring the gospel to the least reached peoples remaining in our world today.

44 A Light to the Gentiles
PAUL

While the apostles ministered in Jerusalem, and while Philip and other believers spread out across Judea and Samaria, God was bringing forth His plans for the man who would be the front-runner in taking the gospel to the ends of the earth. Paul (originally Saul) persecuted Christians prior to his conversion. After his encounter with Jesus on the road to Damascus, Paul had a new mission in life: to be a light to the Gentiles. He passionately pursued that calling. Paul devoted major portions of his letters to God's purposes for all peoples, frequently referencing Old Testament passages. He also focused on going to areas where the gospel had not yet gone, not wanting to build on another man's foundation.

BEGIN BY READING WITH YOUR FAMILY:

Acts 9:1-22; Romans 15:17-21

FAMILY ACTIVITY

Teaching Time: 12 minutes
Materials: Paul cutout (optional), candle for each family member, matches

After dark, turn off the lights in every room except one. With your family, take candles and matches to a dark room. Light one candle for yourself. Then light a candle for each family member. Ask them to take their light to a place in the house where it is needed most and stay there. Dismiss them one at a time, pausing for about 15 seconds between each person. When everyone is in position, go and find them. Ask each person to explain their location choice. Invite everyone to join you in the lighted room to debrief the activity. Summarize how decisions were made and the reason no one chose the lighted room. Share that God invited Paul to join with Him in bringing the good news of Jesus to the Gentile peoples. Just as our family chose not to bring candles into areas that already had light, Paul chose not to stay long in towns where other people were already sharing the gospel and teaching new believers. Paul was always on the move, looking for communities without the light of Jesus.

DISCUSS

1. How did God use Paul to advance the gospel? If Paul were alive today, where do you think God might send him and why?

2. Where is the gospel most needed in the region where we live? How might our family join with God in bringing the hope of Jesus to the people there?

PRAY

Pray that God will make your family like lights who bring the hope of Jesus to others.

45 Gentiles Receive God's Spirit
CORNELIUS AND PETER

Peter and Cornelius came from different regions, cultures, and religious backgrounds. Were it not for God's intervention, they would never have crossed paths or associated with one another. Each received a vision from the Lord that helped remove barriers separating them. God used Cornelius' vision to direct him to Peter in a far-away city. God used Peter's vision to prepare him to accompany a Roman Gentile and share the good news of Jesus with his entire household. After Cornelius shared about his encounter with the Lord, Peter replied, "I now realize how true it is that God does not show favoritism but accepts men from every nation who fear him and do right." While Peter began sharing the gospel, the Holy Spirit came on all who heard the message. Those believers who had come with Peter were shocked that the Holy Spirit had been poured out on the Gentiles! Peter baptized them, and these new Gentile believers were welcomed into the Kingdom.

BEGIN BY READING WITH YOUR FAMILY:

Acts 10

FAMILY ACTIVITY

Teaching Time: 15 minutes
Materials: Peter and Cornelius cutouts (optional), six plastic bottles of similar size, six small pieces of paper, pen, tape (optional), small ball

Set the bottles close together in a triangle formation--three in the back, two in the middle, and one in front. Work together to think of six barriers (physical, cultural, or spiritual) that prevent believers from sharing the gospel or unbelievers from responding to the gospel. Write one barrier on each piece of paper. Attach one piece of paper to each bottle with tape (or place one piece of paper beneath each bottle). Stand about 3-4 m (10-12 ft) from the bottles. Take turns rolling the ball to knock them down. Reset bottles for each person. Afterwards, discuss who needed more than one try to knock them all down. Hold up the ball and compare it to our prayers. When we pray, God begins to knock down and remove barriers to the gospel. Just like we needed to continue rolling the ball to knock down every bottle, it will take ongoing prayer to remove barriers to the gospel.

DISCUSS

1. How do barriers like geography, language, tradition, or religious beliefs keep the gospel from spreading? How did God remove barriers that kept Cornelius from hearing the gospel?

2. Read Colossians 4:3. How did Paul ask believers to pray for him? How can our family pray in the same way for goers (cross-cultural workers) today?

PRAY

Choose one country or culture where many people do not have access to the gospel. Pray that God will remove barriers that keep them from hearing and responding to the good news of Jesus.

46 Gentile Realization
PETER AND BARNABAS

When some believers criticized Peter for associating with Cornelius, Peter gave them an eye-witness account of what had happened in this Gentile's home. After hearing Peter's story, they had no further objections and praised God, saying, "So then, even to the Gentiles, God has granted repentance that leads to life." Meanwhile in Antioch, a few believers began sharing the message of Jesus with Greeks. A great number believed and turned to the Lord. News spread back to the church in Jerusalem and the leadership sent Barnabas to investigate. Once in Antioch, Barnabas confirmed the evidence of God's grace among the Greeks. Then Barnabas traveled to Tarsus to find Saul (Paul) and enlist his help. Working together, these two men met with and taught the new believers in Antioch for a whole year.

BEGIN BY READING WITH YOUR FAMILY:

Acts 11:1-26

FAMILY ACTIVITY

Teaching Time: 15 minutes
Materials: Peter and Barnabas cutouts (optional), six pieces of paper, pen or pencil

Beforehand, create four rule signs with simple instructions (such as: count to ten, hop eight times, clap your hands, name your favorite food). Make two additional signs labeled "me" and "God." Gather your family together. Invite a child to lay the "me" card on the ground or floor. Invite another child to place the "God" card about 4.5 m (15 ft) away. Explain that early believers came into a relationship with the true God the same way that we do, through their faith in Jesus. Then, invite your family to walk from "me" to "God". Next, explain how Jewish background believers in the early church thought that Greeks and other Gentiles needed to not only trust in Jesus, but also follow Jewish rules and laws before they could know God. Invite your family to walk from "me" to "God" again, but this time include the rule signs you created along the way. Read and complete the instructions on each card before proceeding.

DISCUSS

1. In our activity, what was blocking our pathway the second time? How were the Jewish believers making if difficult for the Gentiles and Greeks to begin a relationship with the true God?

2. Read John 14:6. Who is the only pathway to God the Father? How does this plan demonstrate God's heart for Greeks, Gentiles, and all peoples to come to know Him?

PRAY

Praise God for creating one way for all peoples to come to Him-through Jesus, the Savior of the world.

47 Gospel Decisions
JERUSALEM COUNCIL

To help settle the issue of Gentiles needing to follow the Jewish law to be saved, Paul and Barnabas were sent to Jerusalem to meet with the apostles and brothers there. They shared amazing reports of how God had opened the door of faith to the Gentiles. Still, some believers among the Pharisees argued that Gentiles could not be saved unless they were circumcised and kept the law of Moses. After much discussion, the apostle Peter testified to what God had already shown them about the Gentiles being saved. Quoting from Amos, James confirmed that what God had shown Peter also matched what the prophets of old had written. At this crucial meeting, the longevity of the gospel was defined. Because the apostles were obedient to what God had shown them about the Gentiles, salvation by grace (not works) prevailed. The gospel was free to spread cross-culturally. It was decided, once and for all, that Jesus was the Savior of the world, and His salvation was good news for all people!

BEGIN BY READING WITH YOUR FAMILY:

Acts 15:1-21

FAMILY ACTIVITY

Teaching Time: 10 minutes
Materials: Jerusalem Council cutout (optional), heavy backpack or suitcase, Bible

Build a simple obstacle course. Take turns going through it, carrying a heavy backpack. Repeat the course, carrying only a Bible. Which trip was easier and why? Explain that some Jewish-background believers thought the new Gentile churches should be exactly like theirs. Show the backpack as you explain how they tried to carry their own ideas about what a church should be like into a new culture. Work together to think of ideas and traditions that modern-day believers might try to bring along when planting new churches among unreached people groups. Now hold up the Bible as you explain a different way of starting new churches: helping new believers make decisions about what a church should look like in their culture based on truths from God's Word. The Council at Jerusalem was a very important meeting to decide between these two ways of starting new churches. Through the Holy Spirit, God directed the apostles and other leaders to decide that people are saved by grace alone and that God's Word is the most important guide for new believers.

DISCUSS

1. How might churches in other cultures be different from your local church? Discuss the setting, the people, and parts of the worship service.

2. What should be true of every church? Discuss what is essential and what is non-essential.

PRAY

Ask God to give goers (cross-culural workers) wisdom in planting churches in new cultures in a way that focuses on the truths of God's Word and the leading of God's Holy Spirit.

The Unknown God
PAUL IN ATHENS

While in Athens, Paul was disturbed by numerous idols that filled the city. In fact, Athens had more idols than any other city in Greece. While looking at their objects of worship, Paul noticed a statue to an unknown God. As Paul preached, he used this statue to build on the knowledge of the Greek philosophers who were questioning him. Paul did not introduce a new god, but revealed the true God that was unknown to them. Paul taught the people of Athens that God made from one man every nation of men, so that they should inhabit the whole earth (just as God told them to Genesis 1!). Paul also shared that God determined the time and place they would live. Paul explained why God did this--so that all men might seek Jesus!

BEGIN BY READING WITH YOUR FAMILY:

Acts 17:16-34

FAMILY ACTIVITY

Teaching Time: 20 minutes
Materials: Paul cutout (optional); current newspaper, TV, or radio; world map

Set aside a time this week to focus on a current world event that might cause unbelievers to seek God. Call your family together and share that just like in Paul's day, God still determines the times and places that people live today. There are two reasons God put people on the earth at this time in history: to learn about Jesus or to help others learn about Jesus. As a family, read, watch, or listen to a news report. Choose one world event to discuss in a simple way. Locate where this event is taking place on a world map. Talk about how circumstances might cause unbelievers affected by this event to seek God. How might God use believers to share Jesus with those who seek God as a result of this event?

DISCUSS

1. Why did God place Paul in Athens in New Testament times? How did Paul use what was happening around the people of Athens to point them to Jesus?

2. God placed our family in __ (insert your country) in __ (insert the current year). What is happening around us that might cause people to seek God? How might God use our family to point people to Jesus?

PRAY

Ask God to give your family boldness in sharing Jesus with those who seek Him in this generation.

Gospel Multiplies Throughout the Gentile World
PAUL AND TIMOTHY

Paul was clear on his mission to be a light to the Gentiles. He went on three missionary journeys from AD 46-57 and continued to preach even on his final trip to Rome. Paul helped plant and establish churches all across Arabia and Asia, teaching believers how to faithfully follow the Lord and be about His purposes. How was this possible? Paul used the strategy of multiplication. As he encountered potential spiritual leaders in his travels, Paul invited them to serve with him. One example is Timothy. Paul took this young believer along on his second missionary journey. Timothy became his beloved son in the faith, co-laborer in spreading and defending the gospel, and a young church leader. Paul instructed Timothy to pass on what he had learned from him to reliable people—who would then teach others the same things.

BEGIN BY READING WITH YOUR FAMILY:

Acts 16:1-5;
Philippians 2:22;
1 Thessalonians 3:2;
1 Timothy 4:12-13;
2 Timothy 2:1-2

 FAMILY ACTIVITY

Teaching Time: 15 minutes
Materials: Paul and Timothy cutouts (optional)

Explain that the job of sharing about Jesus and teaching new believers was too big for Paul to do by himself. He needed dependable helpers who loved Jesus. To demonstrate Paul's method of training Timothy and others in ministry, choose one parent to be Paul and one child to be Timothy. Remaining family members should spread out in different parts of the room. First Paul should teach Timothy a series of five silly motions. Once Timothy can do the actions, he can go to another family member and teach him the motions. Continue this pattern with the newest learner going to a new location and teaching someone the motions. When finished, spread out around the room and do the motions together. Imagine that each part of the room is a different area of the world. How would Paul's way of training helpers cause the gospel to spread faster and further? Emphasize that Paul and Timothy were careful about choosing helpers. They only chose reliable believers who would pass on what they had learned to other believers who could teach others … who would teach others … who would teach others. This is how the early church grew and multiplied.

 DISCUSS

1. In our activity, Paul was the first person in this chain of believers. Read 1 Corinthians 11:1. Who was Paul relying on as his example? What does this teach us about the kinds of people in our own lives that we should choose to follow and emulate?

2. What instructions did Paul give Timothy in 2 Timothy 2:2? How does multiplication reach more people with the gospel? How can our family pass on the truth of the gospel?

 PRAY

Pray that God's Word will spread rapidly to the remaining unreached peoples of the world.

Believer's Responsibility
PAUL'S EPISTLES

Paul helped believers grow and stay true to the Lord by writing letters that were circulated among churches in a certain city or region. In these letters, Paul continually reminded believers of their responsibility to join in God's purposes of blessing all the families of the earth. Paul explained that as Abraham's spiritual children, believers become heirs who enter into the covenant promise God made to Abraham and his descendants (Genesis 12:1-3). God's promise to Abraham, passed down from generation to generation until the coming of Jesus, is now passed on to each of us. As believers, we are recipients of promise and also have a part in its continued fulfillment. We are instruments to extend God's blessing to all the peoples of the earth.

BEGIN BY READING WITH YOUR FAMILY:

Genesis 12:1-3; Galatians 3:6-9, 26-29

FAMILY ACTIVITY

Teaching Time: 15 minutes
Materials: Paul and All Believers cutouts (optional), small treat for each family member (piece of candy, gum)

To demonstrate that believers not only receive God's blessings, but are to pass them on to others, try this activity. Invite all family members to sit next to each other in a row. Hand treats to the first person in the row and direct him to pass all of them to the next person. The second person should take one treat and pass the rest to the third person. Continue in this way. After the last person in the row takes a treat, have him walk to first person in the row and give him the remaining treat. Emphasize how God gave us something much more important than a treat. Why is Jesus our biggest blessing? Connect the activity of passing the treats down the family row with God passing His promise of blessing down through generations of Abraham's family. Jesus was born into the family line of Abraham and became the Savior of the world. Just like each of us got to receive a treat and pass on a treat to someone else, as spiritual children of Abraham, we are people who both receive God's blessing of salvation and people who pass on God's blessings to others.

DISCUSS

1. Galatians 3:8 says this about Abraham and his descendants: "All nations will be blessed through you." Replace "all nations" with your family's name in the verse. How is our family blessed by the fulfillment of God's promise to Abraham?

2. Think about "All nations will be blessed through you" in a different way. This time, replace "you" with your family's name. As Abraham's spiritual descendants, how can our family join with God in continuing to fulfill His promise to bless all the nations?

PRAY

Ask God to give your family practical ways to bless the nations.

A New Kingdom of Priests
OUR PART IN GOD'S STORY

In Peter's first letter, he makes a connection between God's purpose for Gentile believers in the early church and God's purpose for the people of Israel. God called the Israelites to be a chosen people, a kingdom of priests (Exodus 19). Now, through Jesus Christ, believing Gentiles have received God's mercy and been grafted into God's family. Using language that echoes the Exodus 19 passage, Peter writes that we, too, are God's chosen people, a kingdom of priests, that we may declare His glory (nature, character) to the whole world. God invites each of us to be a part of His story.

BEGIN BY READING WITH YOUR FAMILY:

1 Peter 2:9-10

FAMILY ACTIVITY

Teaching Time: 10 minutes
Materials: blank cutouts for each adult and child in your family, scissors, markers or crayons, a rope or string for your timeline, clothespins or something to attach your cutouts to the timeline

Print and cut out a people outline for each member of your family. Have everyone write their name on their cutout and color the cutout to look like them. Remind your family that God has chosen them to join with Him in what He is doing in the world. Invite each person to attach his finished cutout to the timeline alongside all of the other characters in God's story. As you attach your cutout say, "I am part of God's story."

Option: If you are not using the downloadable character cutouts or timeline idea, have each family member draw and color a picture of himself and write his name on the picture. Open your Bible to 1 Peter 2:9-10 and remind your family that God has chosen them to join with Him in what He is doing in the world. Invite each person to place their picture on top of the open Bible and say, "I am part of God's story."

DISCUSS

1. Read Ephesians 2:10. What were we created to do?

2. Read 1 Timothy 4:12 What does this say about people who are young? How can children be part of what God is doing in the world today?

PRAY

Pray that God would show each of you how you best fit into what He is doing in the world.

52 The Purchase and the Promise
THE END OF THE STORY

In Revelation, God makes sure we know how His story will end. One day in the future, believers from every nation, tribe, people, and language will stand before God's throne in heaven. No group will be missing. They will join together in worshiping Jesus, the one who paid for their sins at the cross! God's promise to Abraham—to bless all nations through him (Genesis 12:3)—will be fulfilled completely. Until that glorious day, God is still at work through His Church, accomplishing the task. He is using us to bring His kingdom to the peoples of the earth, leading them into worship of the Savior of the world.

BEGIN BY READING WITH YOUR FAMILY: Revelation 5:9; 7:9-10

FAMILY ACTIVITY

Teaching Time: 15 minutes
Materials: Worshippers From all Nations cutout (optional), paper, pencils or pens, crayons or markers

Talk about being invited to a party or a special event. Let each person share his experience. Explain that God invites everyone who believes in Jesus to join Him in heaven forever and ever. How exciting it will be to see people there from every culture, celebrating and praising God and His Son, Jesus, together! Share with your children that around the world today, some people groups do not know about God's invitation and that no one has come to share the gospel with them yet. As a family, think of specific unreached people groups. Then make invitations for them to join heaven's worship party. Write the name of an unreached people group on each invitation.

DISCUSS

1. How do you think this heavenly celebration will look and sound? What did the Lamb (Jesus) do to make this celebration possible? Read Matthew 24:14. What is yet to happen before this celebration takes place?

2. What are ways that our family can join with God in getting the good news of Jesus to unreached peoples?

PRAY

Hold your finished invitations. Praise God for His faithfulness to bring people from every nation to know and worship Him.

SUPPLEMENTAL ACTIVITIES

Create your own Bible character timeline & memory verse cards

Print & cut out free **Bible character outlines** from the 52 devotionals in *One Big Story*. Children can follow along as you learn about each of these supporting characters in God's big story!

Print, cut out, and fold **memory verse cards** that will help your family hide the Word of God in your hearts.

Download printouts at weavefamily.org/StoryActivities

YOUR FAMILY HAS A PART TO PLAY IN GOD'S BIG STORY

Don't miss it. Live it out together with *The Big Story Series*.

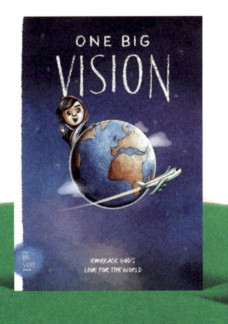

DISCOVER GOD'S PURPOSE IN HIS WORD THROUGH 52 BIBLE STORIES THAT SHOW HIS LOVE FOR ALL PEOPLES.

EMBRACE GOD'S LOVE FOR THE WORLD THROUGH INTERACTIVE LESSONS ON WORLD RELIGIONS AND UNREACHED PEOPLE GROUPS.

EXPLORE YOUR FAMILY'S ROLE IN GOD'S STORY AND LEARN TO LIVE IT OUT IN EVERYDAY LIFE.

Purchase the entire Big Story Series *or download for free at* weavefamily.org/BigStorySeries

One Big Story: Discover God's Purposes in His Word
from the *Big Story Series*

Copyright © 2018 Center for Mission Mobilization

Published by CMM Press
P.O. Box 3556
Fayettteville, AR 72702
cmmpress.org

Printed in the United States

First Edition, First Imprint, 2018

C: 07-27-17 M: 09-19-18 3:28 PM

All rights reserved.

One Big Story is a resource of the Center for Mission Mobilization. mobilization.org

Weave is a ministry of the CMM that exists to connect everyday families to the global story of God.

Weave would like to thank nine global partners who provided valuable feedback and cultural insight in the development of these resources and 14 families from seven different countries who field-tested selected activities in their homes.

We desire to make this material available to as many as will use it around the world in a way that honors everyone involved in the work. If you would like to translate or adapt this resource to use in your cultural context, we are very open to collaborating with you. There are guidelines for translators at mobilization.org/translation.

Please contact us at resources@mobilization.org.

ISBN: 978-1-947468-28-3

Printed in the United States of America.